GUILD LEADERSHIP

GUILD LEADERSHIP

LESSONS FROM THE VIRTUAL WORLD

Jeon Rezvani

Guild Leadership

ISBN 978-1-4357-3955-0

Published by Lulu

To Taresa and Brookie B.,

I love you both more than you will ever know.

Contents

ACKNOWLEDMENTS

There are many people to whom I want to express my appreciation for contributing in various ways to my wonderful online gaming journey: first, to my Uncle Jon, for introducing me to computers; to the gamers who have influenced me through the years: Lalligos, Djarn, Myth, Dantes, Nightmare, Ertic, Soyer, Ironuzak, Shaihulud, Yendor, Vanidor, Lazloth, Phoenix, Nads, Frozboz, Zogg, Jade, Rath, Megaboz, Sevatear, Azrael, Kalaran, Ender, Ravaillac, Axhine, TKD, Chakka, Phyre, Mechzilla, Omni, and Shirak; to the gaming community and to the MMORPG companies, for creating such a great atmosphere of entertainment; to Ken Ewing, for his graphic artist expertise; to Praveen Sharabu, my current manager, for influencing me to write this. Finally, and most importantly, special thanks to my immediate family for molding me into who I am today: my father, my mother (also, thanks for editing this), my sister, my wife, and my daughter.

-Jeon Rezvani, a.k.a.

Krendal, Llort, Jovian, Oidar, Cricket, Gellig, Mortuus, Nubrigol, et al

INTRODUCTION

The primary purpose of this book is to share leadership lessons that I have learned from playing online games and to show how these lessons might apply to the real world.

There are a variety of other reasons for offering these insights and observations:

- To elaborate on some of the similarities and differences between leadership in online games and the real world.

- To give some insight into that with which future generations of leaders will need to become familiar and comfortable, as technologies continually trend towards greater collaboration over the internet.

- To dispel the myth that games are a complete waste of time.

- To give some perspective on a world into which many have never ventured.

- To influence today's and tomorrow's leaders.

My main goal is simply to communicate leadership lessons that I have learned from online gaming.

As you read through the various gaming situations and the leadership skills utilized, take a moment to reflect on the potential applications in your daily life.

CHAPTER 1: LEADERS

What is leadership? Who are the real leaders? What is effective
leadership? What do leaders do? What behavioral traits do
leaders exhibit? In this chapter, I hope to answer these and
other foundational questions.

Leaders Are Influence Change Agents

Online gaming led me to conclude that, at its core,
leadership is all about the ability to influence change. Whether I
was attempting to convince a recruit to join my guild (which is
an association of players, similar to a team or a company) or
persuading a group of people on an expedition to take a chance
on a new strategy that I was proposing, everything always came
down to influencing a change.

For the most part, when I say "online gaming," I am referring to massively multiplayer online role-playing games (MMORPGs). An MMORPG is a game played over the internet by hundreds to thousands of players connected simultaneously in a persistent world based on a theme (e.g., fantasy, science fiction, etc.). What started as Dungeons and Dragons in the 70s, using pen and paper, has evolved into intricate, multi-player, online 3D gaming universes. Please read Appendix A for more context.

The guild leader in MMORPGs is equivalent to a functional CEO in a corporation. The buck stops at the guild leader. He or she can have a variety of responsibilities, from establishing the organizational reporting structure of officers to being the overall compass that guides all the activities of the guild.

Change can happen in a plethora of ways. It happens directly, through avatar-to-avatar interactions, or indirectly, simply because of something that someone has done or said. Ultimately, leaders are always pushing for change. If you don't need change, you don't need a leader. Guild leaders are never happy with remaining static. They always focus on going farther and faster; on heading deeper into the dungeon; on gathering more resources; on making guild members more powerful. One can readily see the parallels in the real world where leaders focus on going farther and faster, on heading deeper into complex challenges, etc.

Sometimes guild leaders need to influence their members to perform mundane tasks such as resource gathering.

For example, building a warship might require a thousand units of a rare and difficult-to-harvest timber resource. Dozens of members might have to spend countless hours of wandering in a sparse online environment in search of a specific type of tree, which they then must successfully chop down. Another thousand pieces of rope might need to be sewn from the hides of extremely rare beasts. Hundreds of playing hours are required by woodworking craftsmen just to attain the proper amount of skill needed to combine the various resources into a warship.

Most people don't find those sorts of rote activities enjoyable, yet they desire the end product – a massive warship – which brings them shared prestige in the community and enables them to engage in ship-to-ship combat (or simply allows them to travel efficiently through oceans). Without someone at the proverbial helm to lead and organize this effort, nothing of that magnitude can be accomplished. Literally thousands of online hours can be expended towards creating such a vessel.

Another example of influence might materialize when a guild leader realizes that his guild is lacking a certain archetype role (perhaps they are short on healers). He needs either to recruit a new person to join the guild or to convince an existing guild member to set aside his or her current character in favor of creating a character that the guild "needs." The same is true in the real world. It isn't always possible to align a person's passions with the tasks at hand. A manager may need to influence an employee to head down a different career path due to what's best for the company and the employee.

A guild leader might need to influence a rival guild to give up its land rights in a certain region. Just as in real life, there are infinite paths at the leader's disposal – from paying the opposite guild to walk away; to trying to embargo their supply lines and making their lives difficult; to coaxing them into merging to become a stronger whole.

Guilds are akin to companies. There are small guilds, large guilds, wealthy guilds; there are guilds that are completely consensus-based and others that would put the military's hierarchical system to shame; there are "hard-core" guilds (those that require their members to invest at least forty hours per week of playing time) and social guilds. Guilds often have officers and constitutions and laws and guidelines.

Guilds generally do not work well with one another (especially when rival guilds are involved), so that leaders sometimes need to influence the "impossible": inter-guild cooperation. The effective leader will develop and pursue successful negotiation strategies with their adversaries.

"Influence" is commonly defined as the capacity or power of persons or things to be a compelling force on or produce effects on the actions, behavior, opinions, etc., of others. That summarizes what a leader does: impel someone to action which causes a change to occur. When that change produces the intended or expected result, then the leader's influence was effective. The term "influence" is to be distinguished from "manipulate," which connotes influencing in an unfair manner.

This leads me to the conclusion that effective leadership is effective influencing, and leaders are influence change catalysts.

The average MMORPG gamer spends 20-25 hours a week playing online games, and another 10-15 hours per week using the Internet for other things.

http://www.theinternetpatrol.com/internet-addiction-not-a-big-factor-with-internet-gamers-says-study

---

Leaders Don't Always Have the Title

The true leader in a guild is whoever wields the most influence, which isn't always the guild leader or the guild officers. The true leader is the person who has the most followers – the person to whom everyone listens during times of indecision. This individual will probably be a longtime, well-respected member or a former officer. He or she might be someone in the gaming community who is well known and usually the one to whom everyone turns when there is seemingly no hope.

Similarly, in the real world, the leader doesn't always have the title. For example, when a computer system is down, the person who leads the people around him towards resolution might be a mid-level employee whose job description doesn't necessarily include resolving system-down issues. Why him? Perhaps he has the experience, initiative or drive, or maybe he has established the trust of his co-workers. He may not have the most senior title in the room, but he is the one who steps up to lead everyone through the challenge at hand. Another example might be when a group of teachers turns towards the most experienced teacher rather than a new principal when seeking guidance and leadership during a time of crisis. I would wager that if Microsoft went into a massive slump, all eyes would turn to Bill Gates more than whoever might be holding the CEO title at the time. Leaders serve because to them, it is the right thing to do, title or no title.

The mean age of MMORPG players is 27.

http://www.gamasutra.com/php-bin/news_index.php?story=6582

Everyone is a Point-In-Time Leader

There are multiple opportunities to lead in massively multi-player online games. The environment is conducive to what I call "point-in-time leadership" or "sudden leadership"; this occurs at a distinct period of time, lasts for a set duration, and is either voluntary or involuntary.

A great example of point-in-time leadership might present itself if the "raid leader" (think of him or her as the General calling the shots on the battle field) dies in the midst of combat (a raid is merely an adventure designed for 10 – 100 players). This could limit his effectiveness to lead (I say "could" because in some games, even if your avatar dies, you are still able to see how combat is progressing and you are still able to lead). At this point, either someone needs to step up and assume that role of raid leader, or if the guild (or group of members) is particularly organized, they have a backup person already designated.

This can happen frequently in the online world, and it is often a trial-by-fire induction into leading a raid. The raid leader is sometimes a figurehead – and his "death" can kill morale. Confusion can quickly set in when that individual isn't making the split-second decisions required to navigate successfully through the battle. If the game mechanics do not allow the raid leader to continue to effectively lead, the participants might instinctively call out for someone else to pick up the reins. "You're in charge."

The medium itself can be the source of the issue – if the raid leader's internet service provider forces a dropped connection, then sudden voluntary leadership may be required. If no one steps up immediately to bring focus back to the battle, invariably avatars will die. This can happen quickly and be for a short period of time – perhaps until the raid leader's connection resolves itself or until the combat is over. The need for leadership often happens faster than the luxury of consensus-based decision-making will allow – a moment's hesitation can cause massive loss. Literally months of work can be lost without quick, decisive leadership.

Assuming the role of raid leader for a set period of time doesn't always happen purposefully. It might be the person who simply wants to rally the troops. "Come on, we can do it!" This might swiftly progress into "everyone concentrate their firepower on the dragon! Forget the others!," or other forms of direction. What usually starts with trepidation can blossom into purposeful action. A leader is born.

Leadership swapping could occur multiple times in the same combat. If the battle has been unsuccessful, someone else might step up to take the reins (generally if the raid leader is still out of commission). There is very little opposition to this type of initiative. People's focus is on a successful raid and achieving whatever goals they had in mind; there is almost no petty squabbling about who is adopting the role of a point-in-time leader. It is well understood that raid leadership is integral to overall victory and it is accepted that people may need to adopt new roles without hesitation.

Player-vs-Player (PVP) raids also have multiple point-in-time leaders. A PVP raid often occurs when one team (designated because of the race they play, not by their guild) goes against another team. The classic breakdown of these teams is "good" races vs. "evil" races, which might be Elves/Dwarves/Humans against Orcs/Trolls/etc. A whole new set of leadership skills can be required to properly influence these giant "pick-up" PVP raids (pick-up because they don't have set participants – just whoever shows up at a certain time). Because these are pick-up games, leaders need to figure out ways to influence action (if no one speaks up, chaos invariably ensues, which often results in a loss). To be successful, proactive and reactive strategy is required. The influential leaders are able to quickly assess the situation (evaluating the people they have, their abilities, their theoretical roles, etc.), and guide the entire group toward certain objectives. Sometimes they may feel compelled to take the leadership role away from someone else, who may be headed for certain disaster. Often, people will want to follow the same strategy that has previously failed multiple times, simply because it worked once in the past. Leadership is key, as is strategy.

Point-in-time leadership happens in the real world as well. A school bus in the countryside careens off the road into a tree, incapacitating the driver. A brave leader among the children somehow has the wherewithal to step forward to help everyone. Perhaps a meeting has veered off track or has stagnated – the leader would be the person who realizes it and acts to get the meeting back on track towards a more productive outcome. The leader is the person who jumps in to right the wrong and, ideally, ensure that it doesn't happen again.

Another example of "point-in-time" leadership is in the recruiting process that frequently happens in MMORPGs. Some members take it upon themselves to identify and recruit (which includes influencing) potential candidates. The online world has multiple opportunities to form impromptu teams to accomplish mini-quests (which are often achievable by 1-8 people). These impromptu "hunting" parties are great opportunities to identify and influence potential candidates (both guilded and non-guilded) to join the ranks. Some people are comfortable adopting this recruitment leadership role, and others are not. That said, most established guilds have officers who are responsible and ultimately accountable for recruiting new personnel into the guild.

MapleStory, an MMORPG developed in Asia by Nexon Group, boasts over 50 million registered users.

http://www.gamespot.com/pc/rpg/maplestory/news.html?sid=6170195

Influence Challenges

I always have been interested in surrounding myself with people who are able to influence all aspects of the game – from the designers who created the mechanics that govern the world, to the community that plays the game. I sometimes would utilize "influence challenges" for potential recruits and existing members to gauge their ability and willingness to influence; I wanted to see if they could think quickly and act decisively in a scenario that they most likely had not previously faced. I usually started with easier tasks, and then, with time, progressed to tasks with increased ambiguity and difficulty.

Generally, I would start with a request that they do something the guild needed – and I would ask if they were up for it. I never liked if they responded with "maybe" or "it depends." I wanted to see confidence. I wanted them to know that they could accomplish what I asked, no matter what the specifics of my request entailed. "Can you gather a party of thirty people near the lair of the dragon in five minutes?" Or, "Could you try to get an immortal to show up tomorrow at noon outside our guildhall?" I also included the reasons for my request.

It was educational to watch how different people proceeded. Some would offer gold as an influence mechanism, operating on people's greed. Others would recruit help to best accomplish their task. Some would coax, beg, or plead. Some gave up. If they sought my input, I was willing to oblige them. It was a great learning opportunity for both of us and was an effective confidence-building mechanism when they succeeded, and they often did.

Leaders influence. In the online world, you strive to influence people whom you have never met. Some leaders in both the real and virtual worlds are able to influence how people think and feel. Instead of forcing their will on others by virtue of position, some leaders are able to subtly influence people to think and behave differently. It's the most powerful type of influence – where the person himself desires to pursue a different course because his vision has broadened, rather than because someone else wanted or compelled him to change. It goes beyond leadership by carrot or hammer.

Some online players of "Second Life" have generated annual revenues exceeding $100,000.

http://www.businessweek.com/magazine/content/06_18/b3982001.htm

---

Change Anything that Doesn't Seem Right

There are no bounds to influence in the world. There are, however, perceived bounds that people arbitrarily create for themselves and which act as self-imposed constraints. My take on this cramping of one's own style is very simple: if you don't like the rules of the game, then change the rules; change the game. If a policy exists in the real world that you don't agree with, work to improve it. If your company doesn't buy into social responsibility, strive to show the business value of adopting sustainable practices.

One area where gamers sometimes feel imprisoned and unable to adequately influence change is around class balance. There is almost always a perception that other classes (classic ones being fighters, wizards, thieves, healers, etc.) are more powerful than the class role which one is playing. It takes a significant amount of time and effort to build a character, so most are unwilling to start over. A common response by players who experience this "grass is greener" syndrome is often to complain, do nothing, or start over. I've been guilty of all three. However, I would always embark on strategies to induce the change that I perceived would yield better class balance. Sometimes that would involve gaining the trust and respect of the designers of the game; sometimes it would involve gaining the trust of the community; ultimately, it was always about influencing the change that I felt was needed to preserve the game's long-term viability and integrity. Striving to rectify any imbalance was always one of my highest priorities.

In the real world, I have seen people feel similarly constrained about their jobs and compensation. Don't be. You have an infinite number of options at your disposal. On your own time, you could learn how compensation was established and then look to grow the responsibilities of your job. You could actively seek out more opportunities for growth/compensation. You could research how you might pursue a different career direction. Etc. If your situation doesn't feel right, then strive to change it.

Time after time in my online career, I refused to accept anything that didn't feel right. Whether it was game mechanics or player-to-player bias, I welcomed challenging the status quo. I focused on doing and saying what I thought was right, regardless of the politics of the situation or what the potential outcome might be. If there was a problem, then it demanded action and change. Whining was useless – it generally did not yield change.

Leaders focus less on whining and more on fixing. They are the influence change agents who make sure that whatever doesn't feel right is resolved. I was never interested in collaborating with people who only complained without ever feeling compelled to influence the change needed to improve the situation. Challenge the issue, don't lose to it.

I was once tempted to leave a modest guild which I had created in favor of joining an "elite" guild that was trying to recruit me. It had the wealth, the prestige, the power. My guild had multiple issues which I hadn't properly addressed. I was ready to quit when the obvious occurred to me – why not just fix what was wrong rather than jump ship? Why not fix the issues rather than run away from them? Why not become the most prestigious guild in the game? That simplistic realization was a defining moment in my online career and also began to permeate my real life. If your guild has an issue, then resolve the issue. Leaders don't need to leave for another guild – leaders strive to fix the issues that they have with their own guild.

There are no limits to what change you can influence. You are limited only by your imagination and by whatever you allow to limit you.

"Don't think you can, know you can."

-Unknown

Key Traits of Guild Leaders

<u>Guild Leaders are Passionate, Positive, and Confident.</u>

I've played with thousands of people throughout my twenty-five-year online gaming career. During that time, I've had the privilege and opportunity to cross paths with countless guild leaders. I have noted a few recurring traits among those that I considered to be exemplary. While not all great leaders possess the same talents or behaviors, they all manage to lead to impressive outcomes.

Great leaders are passionate about their pursuits. They have a strong enthusiasm for whatever they are trying to accomplish. They influence with zeal. They have an intense devotion to leading their people to greater things. They speak and act with fervor. Whether they are rallying their troops when morale is low and all hope seems lost or whether they are trying to focus everyone's efforts on building something, their one constant is passion.

Ask yourself: would you rather follow someone who does not have enthusiasm or someone who does? Someone who is disinterested or someone who is engaged? Would you rather see a movie by a company that makes movies to make money, or one that makes money so that they get to make movies? Passion.

Another distinguishing characteristic of laudable guild leaders is that of focusing on the good, rather than the bad. They tend to dwell on the positive, rather than the negative. I once witnessed an entire guild become annihilated by a deadly dragon. The people were devastated. Some of their equipment was permanently destroyed. Characters were set back hundreds of hours of effort. The guild leader was strangely excited. "Now we know that strategy doesn't work. Let's be the first to find one that does. BTW -- Great job, healers." In everything, there is something positive, and good leaders find that positive.

Confidence is another hallmark of strong leadership. Great leaders know that nothing is unachievable. It is not that they misrepresent the state of things – rather, they are able to envision other paths to success. They know that doubt can be a poison that spreads quickly. Guild leaders who push the envelope of what is thought to be possible, achieving more with less, while operating with confidence, will inspire more from their people. Some encounters in online games are so feared, due to possible setbacks, that characters never experience them. It is only the confident and well-prepared leader that will venture into the deepest, unexplored dungeons. It is the leader who believes in himself and in his people who will ultimately push the limits to discover new areas, uncover hidden artifacts, and define innovative strategies for success.

This is not to imply that great guild leaders are omnipotent or narcissistic. These leaders do not have an inordinate amount of fascination with themselves, nor are they egoists. Not the great ones. The great ones live with humility yet are still confident of their abilities.

I caution against being overly confident. I was at the U.S. Tae Kwon Do Nationals, sparring in the semi-finals. After the first round, I was ahead on points and felt that I would easily walk away the victor. I became less cautious after feeling that my opponent was not my match, and I began thinking of the gold medal round that would follow. My opponent launched into a perfect round-house kick to my head and knocked me out. I learned valuable lessons that day.

9,000 servers globally support the MMORPG World of Warcraft.

http://www.sec.gov/Archives/edgar/data/1127055/000095012306007628/y22210exv99w1.htm

---

Guild Leaders are Assertive.

Leading a guild isn't a passive activity. It requires drive. Many guilds crumble because leadership isn't confidently assertive. It can require quick, decisive, command-driven decision-making – many situations don't allow the luxury of consensus. Inaction often leads to death in online games. Successful guild leaders focus on clear and purposeful communication.

The strongest guild leaders are forceful yet remain empathetic towards people's feelings. They have developed a strong set of values, which allows them to assert themselves appropriately. They know how to express their needs without walking over those around them.

I was once in a guild with a leader who ran the guild pretty much as a dictator. He was effective by many definitions of the word: he had clear goals which people understood and executed on; he accomplished what he set out to do; he always left a lasting impression on anything he touched. However, he was not a great guild leader, as he did not possess most of the more crucial traits. His interpretation of assertive was to be both overly aggressive and threatening. He was selfish and destructive.

Over 1,300 game-masters provide 24x7 customer support in 6 languages to players of World of Warcraft.

http://www.sec.gov/Archives/edgar/data/1127055/000095012306007628/y22210ex v99w1.htm

---

Guild Leaders are Self-Aware.

The exemplary guild leaders know what their strengths and weaknesses are – and they know if they need to work on their weaknesses. They don't let pride impede their progress towards success or however they define winning. A lot of glory rides on the shoulders of the raid leader, who directs the people into battle (which is a primary focus of most MMORPGs). However, the strong leader recognizes when there are more competent raid leaders amongst his people, and he lets them take on that role and win that glory.

I spoke at length with an accomplished guild leader who truly embodied self-awareness. He knew where he excelled and where he lagged. He solicited my input to understand how I perceived him. He understood his own motivations as well as what brought him happiness in the game. He had his own moral code by which he lived (and played). He realized that every decision he made stemmed from his previous collective experiences in life – and that understanding himself better led only to better future decision-making. And he realized that leadership was ultimately about serving others. "But, it's just a game!," you might say. My response is to tell that to the people who are passionately putting over forty hours a week into this somewhat parallel world of human interaction.

Self-awareness is extremely important in the real world. Would you want to be in a car with someone who isn't aware of his own capabilities and thinks that he can drive around a corner at a hundred miles-per-hour? Would you want to follow someone whose ego was getting in the way of doing what is right for the business?

So, the strong guild leader actively seeks input from his people to help identify, in himself, areas where he might improve as well as areas of potency. He wants to know how people perceive his skills. He is self-aware.

"Is Warcraft the New Golf?"
PC Magazine – Jane Pinckard, April 5, 2006.

Guild Leaders are Capable.

Great guild leaders consistently demonstrate that they have the capacity and ability to efficiently accomplish the tasks before them, whether they are leading their guild successfully through a raid, negotiating a significant purchase from another player, or inspiring guild members to push themselves to greater heights. They have the right combinations of skills and abilities, behaviors, and attitudes needed to influence the proper changes. One key difference that I have observed between guild leaders and leaders in the real world, at least in most cases, is that guild leaders are invariably superior at both the skill of performance and the skill of leading. Or, to put it another way, great guild leaders are not just gifted coaches; they are also stellar athletes. This level of competency is often expected of established guild leaders – that they are operationally capable. All accomplished guilds with whom I have interacted were led by an "on the court" leader.

MMORPGs demand that leaders have deep, contextual, gaming knowledge. It is another differing aspect between the MMORPG world and the real world. I've never heard of a guild that brought in an external candidate to lead them. During mergers or acquisitions of guilds, leaders from each guild can take on new functional leadership roles. But I've never seen a guild recruit a new guild leader (CEO) from outside their ranks. And definitely not a leader from another industry. For example, there would most likely never be a guild leader from a science fiction MMORPG recruited to take the helm of a fantasy MMORPG – unless a whole guild was changing games. The reason for this probably has everything to do with the need for both coach and athlete, as opposed to just coach. I always found it easier to be influenced by someone who was proven in the trenches.

> **Over 10 quadrillion bytes of data have left the Sony Online Entertainment Everquest servers in the last 5 years.**
>
> http://forums.speedguide.net/showthread.php?t=139894

Guild Leaders have Integrity.

The definition of "integrity" includes the adherence to moral and ethical principles. Guild leaders who act with integrity live by a personal code of conduct. The types of words that spring to mind when I think of integrity are: trustworthy, honest, fair, having character, to name a few. I have met extremely effective guild leaders who were lacking in some aspects of integrity – for example, their guild philosophy was built on exploiting the system rather than living within it. Some leaders that lack integrity might run their guild as dictators, controlling their people and treating everyone poorly. I never equated an effective leader with a great leader. But both are able to produce outcomes.

Trust is foundational to guild leadership. If the people you support don't trust you, the guild will fall apart. I've seen many instances of guilds rising and falling on trust alone. Delivering on your promises (or better yet, under-promising and over-delivering) is another crucial distinguishing characteristic of exceptional guild leaders which contributes to trust.

Honesty and fairness go hand in hand. If people perceive that they are being treated in an unjust manner, or if they feel that their leader isn't truthful, they will invariably leave the guild. Morale will suffer. A good example is in the distribution of rewards. There are multiple mechanisms that guilds employ for "loot" dispersion. Sometimes the guild leader will make the call on who gets what reward, based on his perceptions of player contributions or based on a system which he thinks will best benefit the guild. A surefire way to lose guild members is if they perceive any sort of unfair bias in loot distribution.

Character. I'd take character over almost anything else, as it seems to summarize so many desirable aspects of guild leadership. The guild leaders who are accountable in all situations garner more trust and respect from the people they support. The guild leaders who feel personally responsible for failures and own up to their mistakes will, again, earn the trust of the members of the guild. I've seen failed guild leaders lash out at everyone other than themselves when a hunt went poorly. Their tantrums ultimately led to their guild's demise.

Integrity and character are also key to all real world leaders. Integrity is one of the four core values at the company I work for (Con-way). It's not just a poster on the wall – it is a value used to guide one's day-to-day actions. Leaders with integrity strive to do what is right, not what is easy. Ask yourself: would you be willing to risk losing your job by doing what you feel is the right thing? I applaud you if you would. Who garners more respect: the leader who never admits his mistakes and doesn't take responsibility for unachieved expectations or the one who apologizes and strives to improve? Integrity. Character. It's foundational to leadership.

> **The total play time for all current characters in Everquest equals more than 184,000 years.**
>
> http://www.gamespot.com/pc/rpg/everquest/news.html?sid=6091457&mode=all

Guild Leaders Listen.

A noticeable difference between guild leaders and business leaders tends to be where they draw the line when it comes to non-business issues. Guild leaders often act, to a limited degree, as counselors, therapists, and even psychologists for the players, and no subject is taboo. In the manner of a best friend, leaders deal with relationship issues, personal struggles, and even issues with addictions – nothing is out of bounds. Candid discussions are a hallmark of the online world. This sort of openness allows for people to quickly build rapport and trust in one another. And in all of it, great guild leaders listen. They are there to listen to players' personal issues as well as in-game issues. Bottom line, they care about their members. However, the more members in the guild, the more difficult it is for the guild leader to really know his people. This is why officers with leadership experience are important.

Real world leaders also listen and care for their people, but, at least in the business world, there are often topics that traditionally are considered off-limits.

Guild leaders spend countless hours listening to the people whom they support. They listen in chat rooms, in private one-on-one instant messages, over private voice-over IP sessions, in email, on the phone, and sometimes, though rarely, in person. The great ones give their entire attention to the person and drop everything else. While most guild leaders have the ability to multi-task very well (because of years of needing to hone that skillset), the good ones realize that it is generally more important to focus on the individual who has a need. In the real world, I have always tried to be the person who stops typing at the keyboard when someone comes to talk to me. I sometimes still regress but am cognizant of that flaw and am striving to improve.

Listening often doesn't require a direct action or response, other than an acknowledgment that what was being said was heard. The bottom line is to respond with what people need (not what you might think they want or should want, but rather what they actually need). It is significant to note, in addition, that when it comes to certain skills, such as empathy and listening, women often are more effective than men.

"There are more than 40,000 unique items for players to discover, create, and buy within Everquest. More than 3,000 of these items have never been discovered by players."

http://www.gamespot.com/pc/rpg/everquest/news.html?sid=6091457&mode=all

Guild Leaders Support/Enable.

Guild leaders constantly are striving to enable their members. They remove roadblocks as possible and they get for them resources as needed. Support can come in the form of: people, tools, items – or it can be less tangible, such as emotional support, time, or knowing that they have the guild leader's backing in their activities.

Removing guild member roadblocks that impede progress toward goals is support that guild leaders frequently provide. A guild member might be resource gathering but might lack the proper tools to be most effective. The leader can reprioritize guild resources to provide the tools which the member needs. A crafter in a guild might need certain components to create items and might lack the right recipes. An adventurer might need support in acquiring a weapon or an armor. All of these types of activities require coordination and support, and it's often the leaders within the guild who step up and help.

MMORPGs are characterized by elaborate quests which require support from multiple players. Guild leaders are often central in providing the support necessary to enable all members to progress on those adventures.

A guild leader's support can come also in the form of providing training or tooling – for example, in setting up and configuring less technically savvy members on Voice Over IP (VoIP) chats. This isn't always the leader, but it is something which the leader must always ensure happens.

As I previously mentioned, guild leaders need to be present for their people. They often provide emotional support for in-game and out-of-game issues. Whether it is a shoulder to cry on due to the death of a family member in real life or because of financial difficulties, or whether it is sharing the trauma of a newly diagnosed medical condition such as cancer – guild leaders deal with it all. Parallel in-game situations can require a leader to provide similar kinds of support to guild members, e.g., helping a member to cope with the loss of his character or lending an ear to intra- or inter- guild politics.

A key to providing support revolves around the simple giving of time. Great guild leaders spend adequate amounts of time with their people. This doesn't necessarily equate with face-to-face (or avatar-to-avatar) conversations. It could be private chats, voice discussions, emails, etc. Most guild leaders like to get to know their people and realize that leadership is ultimately about the people – so they work to ensure that they can spend some time with each individual member.

Supporting, enabling, and being present are all necessary for real world leaders. A team-member might become significantly more productive (and happier) upon receiving certain training or tools. A student may shift into the next gear if a teacher is present when needed. A parent who enables his children to spread their wings and encourages their creativity might be amazed at the results.

Summary

- The leader is the person with the most influence, not necessarily the person with the title.

- Leaders influence so that positive change occurs.

- Guild leaders often never actually meet the people they lead, yet they still manage to build trusting relationships.

- The online environment and the game mechanics themselves create point-in-time leadership opportunities and foster leadership development. The real world also has the same opportunities for people to utilize their leadership skills.

- Influence challenges are great learning opportunities and are effective confidence-building activities.

- Leaders change anything that doesn't feel right.

- Leaders are passionate, positive, and confident.

- Leaders are assertive.

- Leaders are self-aware.

- Guild leaders are both gifted coaches and stellar athletes.

- Guild leaders come from within the ranks.

- Guild leaders often act as counselor, therapist, and advisor to their members on real-life issues.

- Leaders are capable.

- Leaders listen.

- Leaders support and enable those around them.

CHAPTER 2: VISION

What is the role of vision as it pertains to leadership? How do you make a vision compelling? What is inspirational? This chapter will address these and other questions regarding vision and leadership.

Start with your Guild Statue

I've been competitive my entire life. Competition is fun, and I'm clearly motivated by achievement. The multi-player online gaming world was no different for me. I marveled at the players on top of the scoreboards: the wealthiest; the highest character level; the most accolades. I wasn't interested in basketball players, movie stars, or astronauts. I craved hearing the histories of the game from the most erudite players. I mined gaming forums religiously to delve deeper into the lore. Who was first to brave the lair of the dragon? Even better, who was the first to defeat her? Who traveled the farthest into the dungeons?

I became driven by firsts and yearned for topping the leader-boards. Over the years, I amassed many accomplishments (**/boast on**): top ranking in Proving Grounds BBS; first resurrect healer on Sojourn MUD; first chi martial artist in Kingdom of Drakkar; first 50th level Necromancer on Veeshan; helped slay the first dragon in Everquest's history; undefeated in hundreds of player-kill attempts in Mortal Conquest MUD; guild with most wealth and discoveries in Vanguard; and a slew of others (**/boast off**).

Over time, my characters became entwined with the histories of the online role-playing games I played. "Role-playing" is somewhat of a misnomer, as few people actually adopt and act out the role of characters, including their backgrounds, personalities, motivations, etc. Indeed, people are focused more on attaining the next experience level than pretending, for example, that they are a drunken half-giant assassin searching for redemption.

I often liked adopting behavioral traits with my characters. In a few games, I went down in history as the consummate helper to everyone. In others, I was known as quiet and introverted, yet still friendly; in some, I was loud, boastful, and proud. There was no limit to the options and the fun. Early on, I was more of a solo player, but as time progressed, I became more group-oriented. However, while my character's personality changed as I tried different games, I always remained dedicated to supporting my friends and my guilds.

I sometimes revisit games from which I have retired yet still maintain accounts (and the games that are still online), and it always delights me to hear stories about myself or the guilds that I was part of in public chats or in game forums. The more interesting stories always seem to stem from drama and conflict from being in contentious, hard-core guilds.

As my play style shifted from solo-based to group-centric, I noticed that it brought me more joy for my guild to be remembered in history, rather than me as an individual. I remember the defining moment in my gaming career when this happened. I had just completed a long and arduous quest with the help of my guild, and the reward was to be a statue with my character's name on it along with an inscription of my choice. The statue would then be placed permanently in the game. A few statues were already erected, all glorifying the characters that had finished the quest and had opted to honor themselves. People wanted to be remembered for great things – for great contributions.

I chose to forgo the statue of my character and, instead, asked the guild what they wanted. They were delighted, and they opted for a quote from the movie, Conan: "To crush your enemies, see them driven before you, and to hear the lamentations of the women!" Upon reflection, I would have preferred a quote that focused on making our guild the world's best, rather than a negative sentiment towards other guilds.

The guild was so proud that we had chosen the team over the individual. The realization hit me: it wasn't the acknowledgement of my own exploits that truly mattered; it was the acknowledgement of my team, whether I was leading it or not, that gave me (and others) the most joy.

Later, in the same game, when I became the first person in history to reach 50th experience level, the owner/administrator of the game approved a new "Hall of Heroes" to be added to the world. I again lobbied for a guild reward. This time my guild-mates turned down my request for a guild acknowledgement – instead, they wanted my character proudly displayed as the leader of their guild. I complied.

These statues altered how I approached visioning. They added a slightly different perspective to my desire to have "firsts." They introduced the question of what my actions need to be for history to remember my guild. They introduced the question of what my actions needed to be for history to remember my team. My company. My community. Etc.

As a leader, it all starts with asking yourself, "What do you want to leave behind once you are gone?" Don't pass "go" until you figure that out. Start with an end state that is almost unachievable. Once you have that vision (which is what the guild/team/company/church/etc. hopes to become or where it hopes to go), passionately communicate it over and over. As you plan your daily and weekly activities, always ask yourself -- how is this bringing you closer to realizing your vision? One area where I have personally struggled to improve is in communicating the vision. I'll mention it but not drill it in. I always have a vision in the back of my head, but I don't spend the effort to make it known.

Newer and less mature guilds often tend to lack vision. They organize loosely and accomplish little. This is not a bad thing in itself – it is simply how they choose to play the game. Over time, if they last, they tend to develop a more strategic outlook – they think farther down the road and create plans for how they want to get there. They start creating goals for themselves (perhaps as part of an overarching vision of what they want to become), and they begin to organize their day-to-day actions to be in alignment with their goals.

Companies (and other associations of people) tend to follow the same evolutionary maturity. The better they get at aligning their day-to-day activities with their strategic goals, the more they prosper and the faster they proceed towards their vision.

Mature guilds do not lack vision – they create charters, policies, manifestos, bylaws, constitutions, organizational structures, functional departments, etc. They establish and maintain their own knowledge management systems comprised of gaming strategies, item information, location spoilers, efficient ways to level, monster compendiums, quest information, and more. They usually have their own public and private forums with varying levels of authorization based on role. The ambitious guilds have laser sharp focus on who they are and what they want to accomplish. Some guilds are more social, accepting of anyone, and laid back. Others are hardcore, expecting huge commitments from their members.

An example of a guild vision might be to "have the largest guild on the server by next year." They would then focus their efforts on growth. A guild with that vision would realize the importance of marketing, sales, and HR. They constantly would be recruiting, watching chat channels for people interested in looking for guilds, targeting newer players to influence them early in their careers, etc. They would have elaborate web sites and would post frequently in community game forums. They would strive not only to attract players, but also to retain them. They would proudly display their guild numbers and watch their rank increase on game scoreboards of "guild with the most members."

Often in the real world, people do not understand the company's strategic goals. This is often due to a lack of communication or the inability to understand what the vision is trying to accomplish or why it is a business strategy. One of the benefits of the online gaming world is that most people can quickly grasp the vision because of the shared context. Understanding and internalizing the vision generally means that it can more easily be realized. Firsts. History. Chase your dreams. Set goals. Strive, if nothing else. Start with your guild's (team's, company's, etc.) statue.

About 36% of MMORPG players are married.

http://www.nickyee.com/daedalus/gateway_demographics.html

Construct a Vision that is Inspiring

In the game Vanguard, my guild ("Primal") developed the following vision statement: "Our key goal is to become the world's wealthiest guild." I collaborated with two of my most trusted guild members (nods to Vrolok and Frozboz) to arrive at that vision. We were third in the world (across 12 servers) on the Guild Leaderboards, and we realized that we could potentially hit the #1 spot with a well-aimed merge. We also could up the ante and "become the world's most dominant guild." Our definition of "dominant" was the guild having the most #1 slots on the Guild Leaderboards. We merged with another guild ("Pain," the name we also adopted) and hit our goals: Most Wealth, Most Areas Discovered, Most NPCs Discovered, etc. We never discussed this vision with the guild with which we merged -- a mistake, in hindsight. For us, those goals were big, exciting, and compelling. "Dominance" was our theme also when I was in "Fires of Heaven" in Everquest, and it became, for me, a recurring vision in other online games as well.

At a high level, the vision statements guided where we wanted to go. For example, we were second in the world in Most Items Discovered. Accordingly, a portion of our members started focusing their activities to elevate that number. Our crafters slaved to create unique items. Our adventurers explored areas that they had previously blown through because the resources and items in those areas were seen as having low value – but now, they took a fresh look at their discovery potential. Not all of the guild was aware of our activities, but they all understood our dominance. We made the mistake of formally sharing our vision with only a few members – and of not leveraging everyone when creating the vision. But, implicitly, everyone knew that we wanted to be the most accomplished guild in the lands.

Guilds that have strong visions for what they want to become are led by individuals who understand the importance of strategic planning. They realize that vision statements (explicit or implicit) also serve as a way to recruit like-minded individuals, as well as a way to identify candidates that do not align with their long-term goals. Some guild leaders might not think that they even <u>have</u> a vision for their guild – but, if pressed, they generally are able to articulate what behaviors and beliefs they subscribe to and what their long-term goals are; i.e., they know where they want to go and where they "see" themselves being; they simply have not formally articulated it. Mission statements are similar – guild leaders might elect not to formulate a mission statement, as such. They are, however, quite confident that they know what needs to be done to accomplish the goals of their guilds. If vision is the where, mission is the how. Vision also should be both tangible and time-boxed. For example: land the first man on the moon by the end of the decade. Wow.

Recently, I have been thinking that it would be rewarding to focus outwardly as well as inwardly when creating the vision and philosophy for the next guild that I lead – i.e., focus not only on becoming the best that we can be as a group of players, but also focus on making the gaming community and other guilds more prosperous. Go for win/win. It would entail aligning with others who perceive that vision as exciting and rewarding. I have always found it rewarding to help others, but I have tended to keep the best strategies and knowledge for my guild so that they would prosper the most. Perhaps "success for all," the goal of both inward and outward prosperity, will be part of my vision for the next MMORPG in which I participate.

Here are some example corporate vision statements:

Long John Silver's: To be America's best quick service restaurant chain. We will provide each guest great tasting, healthful, reasonably priced fish, seafood, and chicken in a fast, friendly manner on every visit.

Bill Gates (Microsoft's original vision statement): Get a workstation running our software onto every desk and eventually in every home.

Westin Hotels: Year after year, Westin and its people will be regarded as the best and most sought after hotel and resort management group in North America.

Google: Organize the world's information and make it universally accessible and useful.

Put some thought into constructing a compelling vision that inspires your people on the front line to do a great job. It needs to be a vision that makes your customers excited. Only by inspiring your teams and your customers can you truly succeed over the long term.

About 22% of MMORPG players have children.

http://www.nickyee.com/daedalus/gateway_demographics.html

Any Vision Can Come Across Compelling

The delivery of the vision statement can, itself, be a mechanism for making a vision more compelling. The method by which the vision is shared can be inspiring and compelling.

In MMORPGs, professional writers often are hired to construct elaborate histories about the game's universe. Writers create themes, plots, conflicts, and, ultimately, stories that develop and describe the back-story of the game. The writer attempts to evoke a compelling setting in order to immerse players into the game's world. This ranges from stories about the Gods that inhabit the world to the great battles which shape the continents to rumors of artifacts that lie in the darkest lairs of the deepest dungeons. The players become the drama in the story -- drama is conflict in action, after all.

A lot of online players tend to ignore some of the back-stories of the environments in which they play. They focus more on the "hack and slash" aspects of the game and bypass the rich histories that have been created. I, too, have been guilty of missing some worthy content for fear of slowing down my forward progress. Fun for me was leading my friends to dominate the game.

Game histories that elicit some sort of emotional reaction in the reader are compelling. Think of what trial lawyers are capable of when persuading jurors. What are trial lawyers other than master storytellers? They must capture the attention of the juror and lead him emotionally. Movies are the same way – they tend to impact you when they make you feel something: happy, sad, angry, scared, etc. That is not to say that anything which evokes emotion will be compelling or inspirational. However, it can be a good place to start. For example, a quest requiring someone to rescue a blind peasant girl who has been kidnapped from her farming village by a ruthless invading Orc King might be a compelling mechanism when one is trying to influence a group of players to adopt the vision statement, "Our goal is to become knighted as the land's protectors before the year's end."

Leverage the secret that writers utilize in online role-playing games to make environments more immersive, which is to deliver content with compelling stories. Deliver the vision statement with a compelling story (at an opportune time) in order to evoke emotion from the audience. Invest the time necessary to identify actual incidents which support your vision – for example, is there a negative episode in your history which could have been averted had your vision already been realized? Leverage those stories. Deliver the vision and positively influence the audience.

How could "deliver more shareholder value" be more compelling? What if you identified a shareholder whose life savings had been invested in your company's stock and who now lives solely on her stock dividends. Perhaps she is a 94-

year-old widow whose only son was killed in war. This does not mean to lie or exaggerate. It does mean to dig deep to identify stories that illustrate the wisdom of your vision statement. Would that story be something that buoys the spirits of the people around you? Could that story be an influencing vehicle to unite people to lead a more purpose-driven work existence? Will it persuade people to look beyond the issues of the moment and instill a need to work together to achieve the vision? Maybe.

Of course, it is difficult to capture the essence of a compelling story on a hallway poster utilized to communicate your vision. So, start with the gold. Start with the compelling vision statement that is big and exciting. Start with what you would want inscribed on your guild statue. If that falls short, then remember to pitch it with a good story and people might be inspired.

Perhaps, in addition to creating your guild statue, you should create your company's statue; your community's statue; your world's statue. The best leaders should be trying to influence action for the greatest number of people. The environment might be a worthy cause to rally around.

> Online gaming revenues are expected to top
> $3.5 billion in 2009.
>
> http://www.parksassociates.com/press/press_releases/2005/gaming-

Vision, Positive Attitude, and Results are Inspiring

Vision should be an inspiring force that is seen as the preferred future. It should answer the question "what are we trying to achieve?" It should be an energizing and focusing concept which pushes the guild to greater performance and effectiveness. A laid-back group's vision statement might be, "To become the guild voted as 'most fun' on the annual community survey." They would shy away from activities seen as grinding or mundane. They wouldn't require any sort of time commitment from their players. They probably would reward behavior which contributed to their vision. They probably would limit raids which required hours of downtime. This statement and these conditions would attract and retain different types of people – which is part of the purpose of the vision.

I created a guild in a long-running online game that had guilds which had been in existence for years. When we created our vision of becoming the most dominating guild on the server, it got people's blood pounding. Could we become the top dogs? It seemed almost inconceivable. Others were literally years ahead of us – and even a month is an eternity in the online world. We were starting, in essence, from zero. It meant total commitment and excellence. No one could be a weak link. There was some negative history involving certain members of the dominating guilds du jour, which was a further motivating factor. Some of the existing dominant guilds were seen as cheaters (valid or otherwise), so that our vision was seen as "meaningful." It was a choice that we were endorsing. And everyone wanted that dominance. It took us years to finally achieve it – and, ironically, the same perception that we had had towards those others was now cast upon us.

Guilds live and die on attitude. Attitude seems to determine results in online games. The same experience either inflates or deflates the guild, depending on attitude. For example – a "failed" attempt at defeating a nasty creature – the guild leader who chalks up the loss to having learned better strategy invariably raises spirits, relative to the guild leader who gives up or focuses only on how devastating the losses are. The positive leader praises people's contributions in all situations, rather than lamenting problems or placing blame. This directly affects people's morale. I've seen it in chat rooms many times. People can be annoyed about something – anything. The uplifting leader can turn the tide of negativity into hope for a better future. He is able to inspire everyone around him.

The same is true in the real world. The CEO of the corporation I work for (Con-way) held a town hall meeting to communicate vision and results. Even though our results didn't meet market expectations, and the data by itself could have hurt people's morale, the CEO's attitude and his vision for the future were incredibly inspiring. People left the town hall feeling upbeat and ready to tackle the issues, rather than feeling downtrodden and hopeless. There was a buzz in the hallways. It was powerful.

Attitude is also a key part of the influence equation. The best way to change a person's behavior concerning something is to change his attitude towards that something. Instead of focusing on trying to control a person, focus on influencing his/her attitude. I have witnessed that those guild leaders who have a positive attitude tend to influence results more frequently. Guild leaders know that instead of location, location, location, it's attitude, attitude, attitude.

Attitude goes beyond the guild leader. Among the people whom I have led over the years, those having negative attitudes seemed to suffer from a higher likelihood of depression and stress. They seemed to stay home from work/school/etc. more often, due to being ill or simply unable to function. I'm not talking about debilitating permanent illness – I simply mean that the frequency with which they caught colds or other minor discomforts seemed higher. One wondered, was the negative attitude a byproduct of the cold, or was the cold a byproduct of the negative attitude? Positive attitude can be pervasive – the problem is that negative attitude can, too. And the guild leader who generally has the most influence is the one with the greatest ability to affect everyone by his attitude. Attitude affects morale. It affects teamwork. It affects retention. It ultimately affects bottom line results that guilds are trying to achieve.

As someone who loves to lead people, and as someone who is confident that he can influence appropriate change, I've always striven to coach people who have negative attitudes – especially if they were key performers in the guild. It was a worthy challenge, and I always wanted to keep talent. The problem here was that while I found it personally rewarding to coach a difficult but brilliant guild member, the team often preferred attitude over brilliance. It was more damaging to the team to keep someone with a negative attitude than to let him go. Talent was sometimes not enough.

A positive and confident guild leader is inspiring. The bleaker the scenario looks, the more important it is for the guild leader to be optimistic. Again, this does not mean to misrepresent the situation or to pretend that everything is wonderful. But, the leader must have enough confidence in himself and his people to realize and to project that they will succeed in the long run.

Where does positive attitude come from? For me, it comes simply from dwelling on the positive, rather than the negative. Every circumstance can be looked at from whatever perspective you choose. Don't let it control you -- you must control yourself. When I first started playing online games, if something bad happened, it consumed me. I was annoyed if the competition was ahead of me. My thoughts would linger on what I wasn't able to accomplish. As I matured, my perspective began to change. I realized that each mistake I made was an incredible learning opportunity. If a competitor was better at something, I found it exciting to know that there was something I could do to improve. If my character (avatar) was destroyed, it gave me the opportunity to build an even stronger one given my new knowledge of the game. I realized that everything came down to perspective and how you chose to look at a situation. If you concentrate on why it's bad, it will only become worse. If you focus on the good, things will become better because you will make them better.

This way of looking at things has permeated my real life, as well. I had open heart surgery when I was 33. I went in for a routine medical check-up and was told that I needed to see a cardiologist immediately – this came as a huge surprise since another hobby of mine was physical fitness. The heart murmur that was diagnosed when I was eighteen apparently had turned south. The doctor told me that I was like one of those basketball players that runs down the court and suddenly falls over dead. He told me (and motioned in the air) that I was "going over a cliff" as we were speaking. I had almost none of the classic symptoms – just a powerful heartbeat (which I ironically thought was a sign of a very healthy heart) which I could hear in my pillow at night. He told me that my heart was expanding and that I needed my aortic valve replaced... Soon, or it might never be reversible – or worse. Mortality for the operation was low – "just" a few percent. To this day, I look back and realize how lucky I was that they identified the problem and resolved it. Yes, I've had some on-going health issues as a result, and yes, I need to go back in for further surgeries in the future. But, I'm alive, and that's pretty damn incredible.

Another opportunity for choosing the positive view was the birth of my daughter. My wife was diagnosed with toxemia, and my daughter was born two months early. She weighed only 3 lbs, 12 oz. and was so tiny that my ring fit over her hand and onto her wrist. My attitude determines my feelings -- I could look at the fact that my little premie was in the intensive care unit with tubes stuck into her and find grief in that – or I could find joy that my little miracle had survived. Focus on the positive. It will inspire you and others.

Similar to focusing on the positive aspects of a situation rather than the negative is the conclusion that it is better to be <u>for</u> your guild rather than <u>against</u> other guilds. Being an optimist at heart, it always has been easy for me to find good in any circumstance. However, it has been a challenge for me to be simply pro my guild and not anti others. It is something I continually work on. This doesn't mean that I am unaware of what other guilds are doing – rather, it translates into an effort to focus on bettering myself and my guild, rather than on tearing down others.

The final key aspect of inspiration is achieving the vision; i.e., attaining the results we desire because of our actions. Results are integral when it comes to inspiration. Effective leaders are always setting goals for themselves and their people towards enabling their vision. They create and communicate short term goals, long term goals, guild goals, individual goals, goals to help others, etc. Players in MMORPGs generally have a goal of building their own character. Each time a goal has been achieved, it brings everyone a step closer to realizing the vision. Doubts about achieving the vision quickly become squelched as aligned goals are accomplished. What starts as an uphill battle to achieve a vision becomes a force that is almost impossible to stop. As each goal is checked off, inspiration swells.

Needless to say, the real world parallels are obvious.

My guilds achieved a great sense of satisfaction when we were living our vision of game dominance. In one of my favorite online games, we discovered and conquered areas and creatures literally months before other guilds. Our characters had better equipment, due to our ability to go farther, faster. We solved quests and attained skills before anyone else. We had the prestige. That was our vision, and it took us years to realize it, but we ultimately achieved it. The more we achieved it, the more inspirational it was and the more it pushed us to greater accomplishments. We stayed at the top for years – and finally, and collectively, we arrived at the conclusion that dominating in the game was no longer challenging – which made it no longer fulfilling. We decided to move on – and poof, we disappeared. The majority of us went to a new online game, and thus, our quest for domination began anew. There have been effective guild leaders who were not constantly positive – yet they still managed to lead their guilds to dominating the competition. While effective leaders don't always share the same set of talents or behaviors (for example, while most are positive, some effective ones break this mold) – they do always lead their people to successfully realizing their vision.

Asia will be the largest online gaming market in 2009. Europe will be the fastest growing.

http://www.dfcint.com/game_article/june04article.html

Everything Is Not Highest Priority

To accomplish a vision requires planning and goal setting. Most guilds have multiple goals which they are trying to accomplish: complete parts of quests; gather specific items; grow characters; etc.

Some guilds don't plan or organize efficiently. They progress on one quest, only to abandon it due to interest in another quest. Perhaps a few characters attain a subset of what they want and then move off before everyone gets what they need. This lack of clarity in guild priorities leads to slower progression towards the vision.

Hard-core, competitive guilds have specific priorities. Their goal might be to get everyone into the next area. All of their energies will be focused on that goal. Or, the goal might be to acquire wealth – again, the more people focused on that goal, the faster it will be realized. The more dilution of the main goal that occurs, the more slowly anything is achieved. Often there are multiple things which need to happen and, very possibly, in a particular sequence, so they are prioritized accordingly.

In both games and real life projects/companies, a "priority list" in which everything is rated as "high" is effectively not a priority list. In fact, such a list does the exact opposite of what, by definition, a priority list should do, i.e., indicate the relative importance and urgency of the items on the list. Instead, it gives neither direction nor aid to planning. So, a list of tasks/projects which must be done is just that and should be presented and perceived as such. It is certainly easier at the front end to simply proclaim everything to be "high" priority. However, again, the resulting lack of clarity leads only to slower progress and plummeting morale.

For example, if a business worker has a list of six projects, all of which are "priority one," you have to wonder if those projects are equally responsible for enabling the company's goals. More likely, time has not been spent on looking at the projects holistically relative to one-another and to where the business really wants to go. Any time a new demand exists (a new project, an enhancement, any sort of support, etc.), it is imperative to prioritize this demand to ensure proper alignment to the business's goals. Create a well thought-out list of very specific priorities and label them correctly, thereby streamlining your path to the vision.

Summary

- A vision is simply where you want to be in the future. Ideally it should be tangible and time-boxed, and you should be able to know when you get there.

- Maintain a laser sharp focus on who you are and who you want to become – and align all activities accordingly.

- As you go about your daily duties, pause and ask yourself how your activities are bringing you closer to achieving your vision.

- Vision starts with asking the question: "What will be on your guild statue?" In other words, "How will history remember you?"

- Communicate your vision repeatedly. Communicate your vision repeatedly.

- A vision statement can serve as a mechanism for recruiting and retaining like-minded individuals.

- A vision should be seen as exciting inwardly (e.g., by employees) and outwardly (e.g., by customers).

- The online world tends to embrace and comprehend strategic visions and can realize them more effectively due to shared context.

- As businesses mature, they should become more strategically focused and aware.

- Vision, positive attitude, and results are inspiring.

- Everything at highest priority slows down progress towards achieving the vision.

- A vision can become inspirational if it is communicated in a compelling manner. Best to start with compelling material so that you don't need to improvise.

- Think beyond your own statue to that of your team, company, community, and world.

CHAPTER 3: PEOPLE

Who plays online games? What motivates each generation? How do leaders treat people? How can leaders find out what people need? Should a leader be a boss or a buddy? I hope to answer these and other questions in this chapter focused on effective ways to lead different types of people.

People Behind the Gaming

I've had the pleasure of leading people aged 11 to 81 in online games. I've played with skateboarders, yuppies, doctors, retiree's – you name it, I've led them. I've come to know lawyers, drug dealers, pit bull fighters, football players, mothers, CEO's, janitors, surgeons, graduate students, etc. There seem to be no social, political, or economic bounds as to who is playing online games these days. The only true constraint seems to be the lack of a computer and broadband access. Time is a constraint for those who let it be one. Here are some of the trends that I have observed while playing with different generations of online gamers:

[GENERALIZATION ON]

Retirees/Traditionalists (1900 - 1945). I've gamed with a few from this generation. The "radio generation." These are the guys who grew up on radio and lived through both World Wars – think of Babe Ruth and the foxtrot. These are the "kings of grunting" in my book – I've even suspected some of them of scripting before realizing that they were simply incredibly hard-working. These are some of the most loyal people I've ever witnessed. I have never lost a Traditionalist to another guild, though sadly, I have had them pass away. They truly embody honor and discipline. They work well within defined guild structures and hierarchies and they often seem to respond well to a chain of command – regardless if that command was young. They are perhaps the most conservative of all the generations. I have spent more of my time helping Traditionalists to leverage technology efficiently than any other generation – from helping them install and configure game clients, VoIP programs and Instant Messaging, to helping them resolve their DSL issues. Sometimes, even after they were set up, I noticed that they didn't leverage the collaboration technologies at their disposal. This somewhat limited their ability to communicate with the rest of the guild. I noticed that they, unlike Generation Y, didn't seem to crave my feedback on what we did well or what we could have improved. I've seen more Traditionalists prefer solo play to grow their characters (as opposed to group play) than any other generation. This generation is the least greedy in my book. I often had to coax the eldest folks in my guilds to accept rare and difficult-to-acquire items, which was the opposite of most generations. I respect this generation perhaps beyond all others.

Baby Boomers (1946 – ~1964). I've gamed with more Baby Boomers than I have Traditionalists. This is the "TV generation" – think of The Beatles, Rosa Parks, Vietnam, and Woodstock. They often have a gaming ethic similar to that of Traditionalists, who are both hard-working and loyal. Baby Boomers are some of the best team players – they are competitive, they are problem solvers, and they deal with stressful gaming situations exceedingly well. They tend to prefer grouping to grow their characters, as opposed to playing solo. One trait which I've come to truly value in this generation of gamers is their overall attitude – probably the healthiest of all the generations in terms of seeing the positive in things and not dwelling on the negative. Another is their natural vigor while playing – this generation seems to have more of it than anyone, even Generation Y. This becomes apparent in their communication and in their attitude. Guild ranking and titles matter more to Baby Boomers than they do to Traditionalists. This generation is slightly more open to performance feedback than Traditionalists. I have spent some time helping Baby Boomers adopt ever-changing technologies, though less than Traditionalists. The Baby Boomers who truly embrace and become proficient with technology are, interestingly enough, some of the best online gamers out there.

Generation X (~1965 – ~1983). The "computer generation." My generation. Generation X because we are, supposedly, a skeptical lot. This is the generation which has been stereotyped as slackers and those who desire a work-life balance. I've never seen this to be the case in the online gaming world – just the opposite. They tend to push themselves as hard as others, and often there is an imbalance in their work-life. My goal has been for people to put their real lives always first and then dedicate themselves to the guild – balance, above all. I have heard, also, that Generation X doesn't care about themselves or their future. Again, this hasn't held true in the MMORPG world. Generation X'ers tend to solo significantly more than Gen Y or Baby Boomers – so they often are the players whom I can rely on to perform gaming goals which didn't mandate group participation. In my experience, this is the most likely generation to guild-hop if they don't like their guild leader or if a more powerful guild courts them. Generation X gamers don't put as much stock in rank or hierarchy – they realize that it is all just a game. One defining trait of this generation is their innovation – these are the guys who develop the most creative strategies and are the best outside-the-box thinkers. It is often the Generation X players that bring an entrepreneurial spirit to online gaming – from identifying new market opportunities in game economies to creating new raid strategies that beat the game's intelligence.

Generation Y (~1984 - ~2000), also known as, the "iGeneration" or as Millenials. This is the "digital or internet generation." Speed. Multi-tasking. Those are the hallmarks of this generation of gamers. They are the most comfortable attending a guild hunt orchestrated via VOIP, while at the same time convincing their mothers that they can do their chores another day and all the while be watching an HD DVD and listening to an MP3. They seem to process and react to information faster, probably due to a life of video game playing. I've witnessed this in online combat situations where they are comfortable in extremely demanding environments (where multiple things need to be processed and resolved simultaneously). They quickly see patterns and can adapt accordingly. They seem to have the shortest attention spans and can bore easily with some of the mundane aspects of MMORPGs. They are generally very collaborative, both from a people and from a technology perspective. They appreciate and seem to expect constant feedback – and asking a Gen Y gamer their opinions and factoring that into decision-making is a sure way to garner their respect. If the guild has rankings (similar to military rankings), they don't expect to stay at their same rank for a long time (long to them is weeks) – but I have found them to be most taken with the whole militaristic rank structure in guilds. I imagine that this generation will be the best drivers, the best sharp shooters, and perhaps even the best surgeons, as technology becomes even more pervasive in the medical field – i.e., things that they have been practicing virtually for years. They have been immersed in technology and gaming since they were born. I've also found this generation more ready to take risks – and failures don't paralyze them. Again, I attribute this to a lifetime of gaming where failure happens constantly, yet one can always start again or continue. I've heard that illicit drug use is prevalent with Generation Y – my experience has not seen that in online gamers. There is definitely more "flightiness" amongst Generation Y gamers – they are looking for fun over results. I've seen lots of younger gamers change multiple classes multiple times – rather than pick one and stick with it to become the best. That said, nothing is deadlier than a focused Generation Y gamer. These guys are the future.

Most of the Generation Y players with whom I have gamed were at the more mature end of the age range. We didn't feel that young kids would align culturally within our guild – nor did we want our conversations always to remain PG-13. I did make an exception, once, when I met two young boys who had the right passion, drive, and attitude. They were twins. Over the years, it was gratifying to see them mature. I expect great things of both of them in the real world. Currently both twins are enrolled in college – one of them is attending a university in Texas, and the other is going to Harvard on a football scholarship.

[/GENERALIZATION OFF]

These are, obviously, generalities. But they are generalizations that have grown out of many years of association with a huge cross-section of the gaming world. Everything I write is born of my own experience. I do tend to associate with other goal-driven people – perhaps that explains why some of my observations don't fit the norm, or why my experiences might not align with a scientific study.

Who was the best amongst the generations? I could not point to any one that was hands-down the "best." They all excelled in different areas. Discipline. Loyalty. Chaotic conditions. Teamwork. Ability to effectively leverage technology. Dedication. Speed. The "best" was whoever used their talents the most effectively given their role – so, each generation was "best" in certain aspects.

> **The first computer game is generally accepted to have been SpaceWar!, developed at MIT in 1962.**
>
> http://www.jesperjuul.net/thesis/2-historyofthecomputergame.html

Treat Everyone the Same?

No, treat everyone differently. Each player has his or her own unique needs and every good guild leader realizes the importance of customizing and personalizing his leadership accordingly. While there are some generational trends, each person needs to be treated as an individual. How you motivate, reward, acknowledge, punish, etc. changes depending on the person. Everyone needs to be treated fairly, justly, and with respect, but not the same. Leaders should individualize how they manage, based on each situation and unique person.

Guild leaders occasionally struggle with the issue of helping significantly lower level characters. Some adopt policies of "help anyone who asks." This leads to "twinking," which is when a low-level character has items or resources handed to him on a silver platter, so to speak. Ironically, this is often detrimental to the skill development of the player behind the twink, who never learns the playing nuances needed to survive without powerful gear relative to his area of play. However, it might make sense to twink someone who already had a powerful character and was just looking to start another one. The key points are to distinguish between twinking and helping (some guilds publish twink policies) and to treat each individual and circumstance accordingly.

When I first started leading guilds, I focused more of my time on players whose characters grew slowly rather than on those that grew quickly. It seemed logical – help the people who needed it the most and get out of the way of the others. Slowly, the overall average for the character levels in our guild increased. I also have tried spending time equally between the effective players and the less effective. Interestingly enough, the strategy which often yielded the highest overall average growth was when I focused most of my time on my most effective players. However, the coach in me always found it more personally rewarding to spend time with those that needed the most guidance.

There sometimes is a tendency in the real world to "leave the best people alone," because they are self-managing, don't cause problems and do a good (or great) job. I don't advocate micro-managing your most effective people, but I do recommend spending more time with them to further enable their productivity. Someone following the old adage of "treat everyone the same" might split their time equally amongst everyone (or worse, spend most of their time with those that are under performing) – I propose ignoring that advice.

Guild members usually are judged on their performance, not on whether they have friends in high places. Players in MMORPGs rarely heap unconditional admiration on the guild leader. I've not seen people rewarded because they excelled the most at fawning on the guild leader. People freely share their criticisms of the guild leader and everyone, and over time, there is a gradual desensitization to communication conflict.

I was once part of a guild in which the leader always rewarded everyone exactly the same. If the reward was coins, he would split them evenly. If the reward was other items, he would distribute them based on attendance only. It was an easy and fair way to reward. However, it wasn't perceived as a reward by all. Some players didn't need or want the coins – they wanted recognition. Others cared only about the accomplishment itself. Each person had his own concept of what a reward was. It was easier though, for the leader, to simply split things up. Finding out what people actually want or need, and figuring out how to reward them accordingly, is more difficult. But, at least, asking what people want or need would be a good start.

> "In South Korea, videogame players are treated like rock stars, stadiums are named after videogames and many professional South Korean players make six-figure salaries."
>
> http://www.physorg.com/news110864514.html

The Magic Question

The single most powerful question to ask a guild member is "What do you need?" Or, phrased another way, "What can I do to help you (become successful)?" The question needs to be posed in a positive manner. It can open up a slew of possible responses and can yield significant insight into your guild members' needs. If the response is always "nothing," digging deeper may be appropriate. Sometimes guild-mates may need more time to chat. Perhaps they are unclear on certain raid strategies. Maybe they are lacking an item that would benefit them desperately. They could simply be stuck on some aspect of a quest, and they have not felt comfortable asking for help. The magic question is your friend and it's one of the best tools to understand the generations around you.

I was involved in an online game where the guild collectively decided to pool its wealth and then channel the money to one of our members. Wealth could be spent on training, and training yielded faster growth. The guild needed a specific skill that the member could learn if he was experienced enough. We came to the consensus that 10 million coins per week was an attainable goal for everyone. Time passed, and one individual was falling short.

"My character just can't coin like you guys can. I don't have any area of affect abilities to do the job. I'm just a paladin."

There were a variety of directions in which I could take the conversation, from suggesting possible solutions, to identifying alternative roles that he could fill rather than meet the 10 million coin commitment. But, I decided to go with the magic question: "What do you need that will allow you to get your share of the coins? What can I do to help?"

"Maybe if I had Excalibur."

He needed a weapon that would allow him to kill multiple monsters simultaneously, thereby greatly increasing the rate at which he could gather wealth. The guild worked together to give him the tool that he needed – a rare weapon in the game – which, in turn, inspired him to double his weekly share of goal contribution. Win/win.

The magic question applies to the real world just as it does to the virtual world. I joined a new team in a company once and asked the magic question to all of my new direct reports. One person responded that he had been needing more memory for his computer for the last couple of years – that his productivity would be significantly increased with a minor purchase. I asked why he hadn't asked for more RAM from his previous manager and he responded that no one had ever told him that he could have more memory (nor did anyone tell him that he could not).

"What do you need?" It's one of the best weapons in the arsenals of a leader.

Johnathan "Fatal1ty" Wendel won the $150,000 first prize
purse at a recent online gaming tournament sponsored by
the Cyberathlete Profession League (CPL).

http://www.cbsnews.com/stories/2006/01/19/60minutes/main1220146_page3.shtml

Be Their Boss And Their Buddy

For managers in the real world, the mantra is often "Be a boss, not a buddy." The same is not true in the online gaming world. Guild leaders tend to be both a boss and a buddy. They govern the day-to-day operations of the guild. They reward, punish, and council. They also become friends. No conversation topic is off-limits, and political correctness often goes out the window. They ultimately fraternize with the troops. Indeed, they see themselves and are seen as one of the troops.

Some management styles discourage activities such as playing sports or grabbing a beer with coworkers. There are clear responsibilities that a leader has – it is a role as important as any other on a team. But, usually in the online world, the line between boss and buddy blurs successfully. It happens in the real world as well – think more of Def Jam cofounder, Rick Rubin, or Dallas Mavericks owner, Marc Cuban, than of Steve Carell's portrayal of Michael Scott on NBC's comedy "The Office."

Guild leaders must be comfortable rewarding and punishing based on performance, not on levels of friendship. High-end, results-oriented guild leaders don't play favorites – their focus is on performance and achievement; yet, they still care about the people's real lives behind the avatars. Granted, guild leaders have the luxury of being completely open and transparent.

If a player isn't performing up to standards, everyone will be aware due to the nature of the environment. People die when you make mistakes in MMORPGs. Online death, in certain instances, can set you back months of playtime. Guild members will communicate freely about how people perform – from berating others to offering advice. It would be difficult to distinguish between someone who was a guild leader's real-life friend and someone who was not, simply because within the game, the two would be treated similarly.

Before offering an invitation to join, most hard-core guilds will force new candidates – friend or otherwise – to go through a trial period. This is to ensure that there is alignment between player and guild philosophies and to determine if the player has skill. Hard-core guilds have the unspoken expectation that performance will trump friendship. Yet, those hard-core guild leaders still manage to maintain a boss-and-buddy relationship with their members. If a player isn't pulling his weight or isn't able to show up on key hunts, then that specific guild isn't the right place for that player. There are countless other guilds which may align with a player's particular philosophies and play preferences. This expectation helps cushion the blow if a friend is asked or forced to leave a guild. It also explains why some real-life friends play on the same server but end up in different guilds – they have differing play styles and preferences. People remain friends, but they simply are not in the same guild.

Guild leaders are somewhat like college fraternity presidents. They motivate their members to maintain a certain standard of performance in school; they inspire their members to volunteer and better the communities they live in; they punish members who cross the lines. They ultimately have to make the tough call if a member needs to be kicked out – even if it's their best friend.

A benefit of being both a boss and a buddy is that people understand that the guild leader truly wants everyone to be successful in their roles. When there is an expectation that anyone might give some on-the-spot performance feedback, criticism becomes easier to digest. Trust and respect are easier to foster if there is friendship outside the game and honesty inside. Again, while some effective guild leaders do not subscribe to the "boss and buddy" approach, many of the exemplary ones do.

A Shanghai online gamer was given a suspended death sentence for killing a fellow gamer when he found out the friend had sold his virtual sword (for about $870).

http://news.bbc.co.uk/1/hi/technology/4360654.stm

Recruiting the Holy Trinity: Warriors, Healers, Mages

In online games, there are generally three archetypes of roles (or classes): the warrior, the healer, and the mage. The warrior is your meat shield, taking the hits on the front line, trying to keep the attention of the monsters on himself and away from the less hardy healers and mages. Armed with defensive magic that protects and heals others, the healer tries to keep people alive. Mages (or wizards) are the big guns -- they do devastating damage from afar. There are other archetypes that exist (scouts/thieves, etc.), but the above are the big three. The holy trinity.

In the real world, I see the warrior as the "doer." The programmer or the implementer. The healer is there on the sidelines, providing key support. A project coordinator or an administrator. The mage is often a thinker. The innovator. The evaluator. The researcher. Perhaps an analyst or someone involved in Research & Development. Individuals often span archetypes – e.g., a warrior can be an innovator. Leaders can come from any archetype and are needed everywhere.

When you are building a guild, you need to ensure that all the key archetype roles are filled. When creating an impromptu hunting group, you may need more of a particular type of role depending on the task that needs to be accomplished. For example, you might need to be heavy on warriors and healers, with no requirement for mages. Sometimes you need backups, in case the primary goes down (i.e., dies). For example, if your healer is able to resurrect players from the dead, then who would resurrect your healer if he goes down? Another healer.

In each online game, the most popular class (or role) often varies – generally, it is the class that is perceived as "having the most power." In some games, that might be the warrior. In others, it may be the healer. There is often a purposeful design trade-off between a character's ability to solo and his usefulness in a group (the higher one is, the lower the other is). So, recruiting the roles you need can be challenging – especially if no one is interested in playing a role because its usage is limited. Recruiting is often a competitive endeavor – more established guilds will often attract the best talent. It is common to hear people broadcasting messages on global game chats marketing their guild. I almost never have tried to recruit – I would let my guild's accomplishments speak for themselves.

My philosophy in online gaming always has been that it is better to wait to find a great player rather than fill a role with an available mediocre player due to a need. Average players dilute the power of the guild rather than raise its collective whole. For me, talent always has trumped need. If a specific archetype need already was covered, and an incredibly talented player of that archetype came along, I always have tried to get him or her to join. A spectacular player is too valuable to pass up, regardless of the role he fills. Most guilds close down their recruiting when they have all the archetypes covered: "We don't need any healers, but we still need a few good warriors."

Of course, it is important to not only recruit the best but also to bring out the best capabilities in the people around you.

The online gaming environment is conducive to meeting new people. There are multiple opportunities to form impromptu hunting groups to accomplish quests (which are often achievable by 1-8 people), grow your characters, and foster social collaboration. These impromptu hunting parties allow people to meet both guilded and non-guilded players. During these play sessions, people get to know one another – what goals and aspirations people have; what sort of culture they want to be a part of; are they exploiters or do they follow the laws of the land; what are their play styles like; how often do they play; etc.

When new talent approached me for membership in guilds that I led, I often asked them what their passions were, in and out of the game. Did they have leadership attributes or aspirations? What motivated them? What goals did they have? Where did they want to be in a year? Where would they want their ideal guild to be in three years? Did they like to master one archetype, or was it more fun for them to become a jack-of-all-trades? What other experience did they have? What expectations did they have for others? How much time did they devote to online gaming? How long had they been gaming? Many of these questions would surface over time, as I played with new candidates. Performance was integral to getting a guild invite.

I always had a lengthy trial period before allowing someone into the guild. I was very selective. Once I offered someone an invitation to join the guild, I was confident that they would accept – I had a 100% acceptance ratio. I made some recruiting mistakes over the years, allowing people into the guild that weren't aligned with our hard-core play styles – generally, people who could not perform. They ultimately either were asked to leave the guild or they realized the mistake they had made and left on their own.

With selectivity comes an air of mystery. People perceive successful guilds that tightly constrain their invites as elite. This adds to their recruiting potential and further helps them to attract other like-minded players. The best attract the best. My goal was to recruit only people who would raise our collective average, rather than dilute our power. I preferred lean and mean to bloated and mundane. This allowed our guild to operate with a fraction of the number of people, yet accomplish things that larger guilds failed to accomplish. An incredible player in an online guild is like an incredible programmer – they are not just 50% more effective than an average person; they can be 500%+ more effective.

In the real world, I've interviewed and hired many people. I've adopted many of my gaming recruiting philosophies and strategies: I try to get all the archetypes; I try to hold out for a great person rather than settle for a good one; and if a spectacular talent comes along that isn't quite what I was originally looking for, yet is someone that could really enable the business, then I strive to find a place for him somewhere. I'm still waiting for the day when across my desk comes a résumé that highlights the candidate's online gaming responsibilities.

"In 2001, Edward Castronova, an economist at Indiana University and at the time an EverQuest player, published a paper in which he documented the rate at which his fellow players accumulated virtual goods, then used the current R.M.T. prices of those goods to calculate the total annual wealth generated by all that in-game activity. The figure he arrived at, $135 million, was roughly 25 times the size of EverQuest's R.M.T. market at the time. Updated and more broadly applied, Castronova's results suggest an aggregate gross domestic product for today's virtual economies of anywhere from $7 billion to $12 billion, a range that puts the economic output of the online gamer population in the company of Bolivia's, Albania's and Nepal's."

http://www.nytimes.com/2007/06/17/magazine/17lootfarmers-t.html?pagewanted=3

How to Win Over the A$$h01e

The online gaming culture is an interesting one. People tend to show their true colors fast and hold back less. If someone is dishonest, it comes out quickly. That person on the other side of the 'net probably isn't a playboy model. If someone gets aggravated easily, it immediately becomes apparent. Assholes can run rampant due to the veil that an avatar provides – people often start new anonymous characters. The lax accountability comes from the gaming community, which is generally very forgiving. Memories are short in the online world. Discussions can quickly become heated in global chats, but just as quickly, they fizzle out. Players gradually become numb to the conflict. You filter out bickering and strife.

In the online gaming world, you sometimes need to work with difficult people. Perhaps they have found a resource that your guild needs in order to complete a quest. Maybe they have a skill that is beneficial to complete a goal. Maybe they know a secret strategy that the guild has struggled to identify. There are always reasons to work with people with whom you don't see eye-to-eye.

In online games, there are two distinct roles: players and administrators. Admins are sometimes the designers, the coders, the owners, or simply guides whose job it is to help players. In some online games that I've played (free and pay-to-play), I've been asked to administrate. In some multiplayer online games, both text-based and graphical, I've created content, coded, and designed. I have been a guide. Ultimately, I always was asked to watch over the game to ensure its health. I've been asked to pour through chat logs to find cheaters. I learned a lot about human behavior from watching people's interactions with one another.

The key to winning over individuals in an online game and in the real world is to understand the root motivations for their behavior. Why do they act the way they do? What are their needs that you could fulfill? What pains do they have, and how can you remove those pains? Do they want money? Fame? Challenge? Another big avenue to winning someone over is to respect them. If you treat your worst enemy as if he is your boss, you will eventually win him over.

Figuring out what makes someone tick is key to influencing him. It is key to leadership. The great guild leaders whom I have seen loved to lead people -- it was their passion in life. They saw the best in people and inspired them to greater heights. They knew that leadership was influencing change in people. The best leaders can win over almost anyone.

South Korea has a law enforcement unit that investigates "in-game crime."

http://www.netfamilynews.org/2005_06_05_archive.html

Cut Out the Poison

Nothing spoils a guild faster than teammates that are constantly negative or lacking character. They bring down others in the guild. They can crush morale. They focus on the negative rather than the positive – and bring doubt where, otherwise, there was confidence. They capitalize on less-than-ideal situations and seem to get enjoyment from bothering their teammates. Communication and cooperation deteriorates.

Cutting out poisonous people applies to real world teams as well. An amazing amount of dysfunction can result from a bad apple, just as an amazing amount of function results from good leadership. It is important to differentiate between a bad apple and someone who challenges the status quo. Rocking the boat and non-conforming can spark strategic innovation. The bad apples are the poison, and as soon as the poison is detected, there are two options: make significant effort to turn the person around, or drop them from the guild or company. It is necessary to never turn the other cheek on a problem person. An alarm bell should go off if you ever hear that someone "has always been that way." This simply means you need to look more closely.

I believe that people can change if they truly desire it. It doesn't happen often, but it can happen. For that reason, I give people the benefit of the doubt and always have tried to mentor rather than give up on someone. It all comes down to how much effort and energy you want to spend. However, I acknowledge that it can be like pushing against a wall.

It can be difficult, especially if the person has extreme talent, to do the right thing. I once made the mistake of extending a guild invitation to someone who had a fundamentally negative attitude, but who, at the same time, was the most powerful warrior in the history of the game. I was blinded by the power he could bring to the guild. I figured that I could just mentor him, inspire him to improve, have him work on his weaknesses, shield what was negative, and just leverage the positive. But, I did not succeed. His attitude never improved. He was constantly bringing other people down. It was quite some time before I finally had the conviction to cut him out of the guild. Upon reflection, I wish that I had done it sooner. If someone doesn't fit, get him to a place where he will fit. This experience (and many others) led me to the conclusion that people fundamentally don't change – what you see is what you get, and your focus needs to be on leveraging their strengths rather than correcting their weaknesses. If someone is negative most of the time, he likely will remain negative. And if that won't work in your guild, then he cannot be in it.

Cutting out the poison also applies to cutting out wasteful actions. A slight increase in efficiency can have dramatic affects on productivity, especially if that efficiency comes in a place that occurs often. One of the basic activities in online gaming is growing your character. The classic way in which a player accomplishes this is through combat. Kill 10 orcs. Gain some power and abilities. Then kill x of a more difficult monster. Rinse and repeat.

Being a min/maxer (doing the minimum effort in the least amount of time for the maximum gain) by nature, I always have looked for ways to gain the slightest edge in whatever I was doing. Could I rearrange my graphical-user interface (GUI) so that my macros required 2 keystrokes instead of 3? Could I leverage the natural position of my hands on the keyboard to respond quicker to something happening in the game? What is the optimum way to search for and gather loot? Is it to kill 20 monsters in the same area and let the monsters decompose, revealing their loot, or is it to kill and search one at a time? Do you gain more experience from killing the orc or the goblin? What are the losses you sustain? How far do you have to travel? Is the area in which you are hunting sustainable for character growth? Can you capitalize on those cycles and hunt in different manners? What are the ideal classes to hunt with when playing for experience? For wealth? Everything could be improved. Everything could be optimized.

This philosophy came from my programming background. I was always looking to eek out every cycle of computing performance. To clear a register, the fastest standard programmatic way is to "MOV AX, 0," which would move zero into the AX register in, for example, 10 cycles. But, if you thought outside-the-box, you would do "XOR AX, AX," which might take only 3 cycles (using the built-in math co-processor) and accomplish the same end result – perform the mathematical XOR operation on the AX register against itself – which capitalizes on the principle that any value XORed with itself returns 0. Or, perhaps in a flight simulator, you might need to calculate SIN values for the angle of descent. You could use a sin() function, which might take 150 cycles to return a value. Or, if you thought outside-the-box, you could pre-calculate all sin values and store them in memory, and then do a lookup based on an index, which might take 20 cycles. The key in any optimization was to profile what was happening frequently, identify where the biggest bang for the buck would be for a possible optimization, and take minor iterative steps to improve.

I was never satisfied that I had uncovered the best way to operate in online games. There always were better ways. Nothing was more gratifying to me than to identify a new strategy to perform more effectively. I sometimes met online players in real life, and I always found it educational to watch them at the keyboard to see how they operated. To reduce the time that it would take me to react to a situation, or to increase the speed at which I grew my characters, I always asked myself how I could optimize what I was doing and, indeed, if I even needed to be doing what I was doing. For me, that was fun. For others, it ruins the gaming experience.

My workplace recently has become excited about adopting "lean" methodologies. Lean is a continuous improvement mindset and approach that reduces waste from activities while aligning them to a growth strategy (with a focus on bringing value to your customers). I'm interested in seeing how the min-max philosophy in MMORPGs compares and contrasts to "lean."

---

eBay's internet games section generated revenues of $9 million in 2003.

http://www.netfamilynews.org/2005_06_05_archive.html

Implement Traditions

An effective way to unite generations of gamers in MMORPGs is to implement traditions. It is a great way to foster family and instill a sense of pride. Traditions are excellent online "team" bonding experiences that connect the current members to previous ones. Traditions link multiple generations with a sense of identity and closeness.

In one online game, we instituted one of my favorite traditions when we initiated a new recruit into our guild. We created an elaborate ceremony that was held in a location that was exceedingly difficult to get to (so that most people in the game had never seen it or been there). Fortunately, we had an ability that allowed our guild to teleport directly to that spot. We then decorated the entire area. Each guild member would then line up, forming two columns and laying their weapons in front of them. This created a path for the initiate to walk on, and I was waiting at the end of the path. We cast spells to make the entire area pitch black, and then we would teleport the initiate into the darkness. I would call the initiate to come forth into the night, and once he passed a certain location, we would cast blinding light into the area. Then I launched into a speech about our guild and our philosophies. It was fun and inspirational.

Another tradition that I implemented in a different online game was something I leveraged from my days playing rugby in college. The first time a rugby player ever scores in a game, he must do a "Zulu." A Zulu is when first-time scorers jog around on the inside of a circle of experienced rugby players who are chanting and drinking beer. It is a sort of celebratory initiation into the ranks of the battle-hardened warriors.

My variant of the Zulu tradition was that after we had defeated a challenging monster for the first time, we would jog around it, chanting our guild motto. My avatar would begin the ceremonial circling and chanting, and then the others joined in. It became part of the uniqueness of our guild.

Everyone loved our traditions. It gave people a unique sense of family and belonging. It gave them a sense of identity, which made them proud. The older generations liked it, as did the younger. It was a great mechanism for bonding. I've seen only a minority of guilds implement traditions. That said, sometimes it can benefit a guild to wait and bond on their own before implementing a tradition. It's something that everyone should contribute towards creating, and it can't be forced – the timing needs to feel right.

Traditions should be implemented in real world teams as well. Don't limit special bonding occasions to only your family outside of work. Look to grow the soul and spirit that exists within a company (or church or school, etc.) by implementing respectful traditions.

"At the 59th Emmy Awards Ceremony, South Park creators Matt Stone and Trey Parker were awarded an Emmy for the South Park episode, 'Make Love, not Warcraft.'" (a World of Warcraft spoof)

http://news.filefront.com/world-of-warcraft-south-park-episode-wins-emmy/

Trust, But Verify... Is Not Trust.

Trust, but verify. Ronald Reagan used that phrase when describing the US policy towards the USSR. I think that it speaks accurately to the level of tension in the relationship of the two countries. However, I think that it makes no sense when you are leading and managing people. I've always chosen the position that people are innately good and that trusting others is the first step in establishing mutual trust.

Trust makes things easier to accomplish. It is the foundation for effective and open communication. It helps with retention of guild mates. Trust helps with motivation. It is a precursor for taking risks and for cooperating with others. It is integral to a successful guild or business.

There are a variety of ways to establish trust in online games. One is to share your character's password with your guild-mates (when it's legal to do so). Delivering on your promises is central to fostering trust. Having your guild-mates' backs at all times is also a trust-building mechanism. A great way to show trust in online games is to push leadership positions onto others – let people take on new roles, such as leading hunting parties, and then be there to coach them privately in the background if needed -- let them take the success. Listening and attempting a newly proposed strategy are also effective trust-building techniques. Sharing strategy among guild-mates is a great way to establish trust. These trust-building examples apply in the real world, as well, from delivering on your promises to pushing leadership positions onto others.

In one online game, there was a very dangerous area which was full of powerful NPCs fighting weaker NPCs. As in many MMORPGs, when the NPCs died, they reappeared alive a short time later. This repopulation mechanism allowed other people to enjoy playing in the same area within reasonable time frames. As time went on, the area became progressively filled with more and more treasure which had been left behind by the weaker NPCs who were dying. This was a purposeful game mechanic, created by the designers, intended to reward powerful groups of characters who ventured into this deadly territory.

Through trial and error, I had figured out strategies by which one of my characters could gather loot from this area almost risk free. I learned how the NPCs AI worked; what areas had the best treasure; the fastest way to get in and get out; etc. I was the first person in this incarnation of the game to loot the area – I was willing to take the risk (death by one of these NPCs could set you back a significant amount of time) because of the incredible reward. It was in the early stages of the game, and people couldn't believe the wealth and resources that my character had acquired. The critics came out in droves with claims that I was cheating. I ignored the critics and continued looting, and then I utilized the cash to build a powerful new character.

After I started my guild, I shared my secrets with my new guild members. None of my allies had ever asked me how I acquired the wealth – perhaps because I had ignored the critics who had demanded that I divulge my source. But, I felt, also, that it was time to grow the group over the self. I then created a guild bank and gave everyone full access to it. "Take whatever loans you need and pay them back when you can."

After I had shared that and other strategies, one of my guild members took me aside to chat. He couldn't believe that I had shared the information because I had had the entire area to myself. I explained that my philosophy was that it was more important for all of us to prosper, than just me. Then he warned that someone could simply take all the gold in the new guild bank that I had created. I said that I was confident that this would not happen, as I trusted the people in the guild -- that's why I guilded them. He was still surprised. "What if you are wrong?" (about trusting them). I remember pondering his question. What if I was wrong? What if my trust was exploited? And then it occurred to me. "That's okay. I'll have gained all of your trust in the process."

"Well," he continued, "maybe you could script a proxy to be the intermediary to the guild bank --." He was suggesting that I code something that would monitor and report withdrawals and deposits to the guild bank. I cut him off. "No need. Thanks, though." I decided not to monitor my people until I had reason to monitor them. I needed to truly trust my people – and, in my eyes, verifying what they did was not trust. The mileage I gained from sharing my secrets always outweighed the risk of someone abusing the trust. I was steadfast in my belief in trusting people.

Another example of trust (but not verify) occurred in a different online game. This was a player-versus-player game, in which guilds fought other guilds. We had created an elaborate plan to strike at another guild in their home town. We were hidden outside their city gates, waiting for our newly recruited scout to return from scanning the area.

The scout that we were waiting for suddenly spoke. We didn't even see him return – he had managed to sneak in without a trace.

"Looks ideal. Only two guards loaded. The path is clear. Everything looks... okay I guess."

"I guess?" I typed back.

"Nods. Doesn't feel right. It's too quiet. Shrug," he responded. He was expecting to find "Newbies" wandering around their city.

My teammates were getting antsy. The attack had been days in the planning. People had stayed up late (we were working with folks on both coasts and overseas). They wanted to strike. Patience was waning.

"Let's do it," someone urged. A few others nodded in agreement.

"Maybe you should go check," one of my trusted advisors whispered to me privately.

"Why?," I responded.

"Maybe he's wrong. Can we fully trust him yet?"

He knew that my character, also, could sneak into their city undetected. But, I trusted this new guy. We had an extensive recruiting program; we were extremely selective about who received a guild invite. My philosophy was usually to play with someone for months, sometimes longer, before I made any decision to vote them into the guild. It generally took a unanimous vote of all members for a new addition. I wanted only the best.

This scout was the best of the best. He had maxxed his tracking skills. He could pass virtually without a trace. When things got crazy, he was level-headed. He knew every area in the game. He was a quick thinker. And he had a deadly backstab. I had done extensive digging into who he was and what made him tick. I trusted him.

"You know he wouldn't be here if we all didn't fully trust him," I whispered back.

"Yeah, but you could double-check. You know, trust, but verify."

"I'll double-check as soon as something doesn't feel right. Until then, I'm not going to second guess my mates."

My friend nodded.

"Let's move out." I told my people.

The area went dark as the ambush struck us. The opposing guild was hidden and invisible, waiting in the outskirts to surprise attack us after we engaged their guards. We recovered and barely were victorious. Had we not listened to the scout, we probably would have lost due to the combined forces of the opposing faction's guards and the hidden guild.

If I don't trust someone, I'll get rid of him. I've kicked people out of my various guilds when I couldn't trust them, and in real life, I have fired people who lost my trust. Trust, but verify, isn't trust. This doesn't mean that you blindly give people more than they can handle, but it does mean that you believe in your people until you have reason not to. Trust, and don't verify means that you verify only when you perceive your trust to be shaken, but not before. If you find yourself having to verify frequently, there is a bigger problem at hand. Your instincts will tell you when something is wrong. Trust your instincts and trust your people.

Summary

- Traditionalists are often the best grunters. They are the least greedy. They tend to prefer solo over group play.

- Baby Boomers are some of the best team players. They tend to have more vigor than any other generation.

- Generation X gamers are not slackers; they also tend to have the worst ability to balance work and life. This generation is most likely to leave a guild. This is the most innovative and entrepreneurial generation.

- Generation Y gamers will probably grow up to become the best drivers, the best sharp shooters, and perhaps even the best surgeons. This generation is the most open to taking risks – and failures don't paralyze them. Generation Y gamers do not tend to use illicit drugs. This is the generation that is most likely to try multiple character classes rather than stick to one.

- Treat everyone fairly but differently. How you motivate, reward, acknowledge, punish, etc. should change depending on the person.

- In online games, guild leaders often are both the boss and the buddy.

- Attracting a quality person is as rare in the online world as it is in the real world. Losing that person can be damaging when certain strategies are deeply held secrets.

- Ensure that your team has all the functional roles that it needs. Hold out, as long as possible, for the best talent to fill those needs.

- "What do you need?" or "What can I do to help you (become successful)?" are the most important questions that you should be asking.

- Spend more time with your most effective people.

- Implement traditions to give people a sense of family and belonging.

- People are innately good. Trust them. Don't worry about verifying <u>until</u> you feel that your trust has been broken.

- If your treat your worst enemy as if he was your boss, you will eventually win him over.

- Cut out wasteful actions in any process you follow. Continuously look to be better, faster, and cheaper.

- Get rid of poisonous people – they bring an amazing amount of dysfunction.

CHAPTER 4: RAIDS

Are there parallels between business situations and online gaming combat situations? What do leaders do in difficult situations? Is risk good? How should people be rewarded after accomplishing something? This chapter will explore these and other questions.

Combat Brings Out the Best and the Worst

I believe that combat (and other extreme situations) can bring out the best and the worst in people. I've seen cowardice in combat. I've seen people overcome their fears. I've seen a single character stay behind fighting a boss mob (e.g. a dragon) that couldn't be beaten, to buy everyone else time to escape – he sacrificed his character and his real life time for the guild. I've seen people cheat. Lie. Even cry. I've seen friendships rise and fall, all in intense situations. In the real world, many business situations are analogous to raids. These could be negotiations, projects, mergers, etc. Basically, **a raid is similar/analagous to any difficult situation where many people are striving to accomplish something**.

"Raids" are adventures designed to require multiple teams of high level characters working together (as one large team) trying to overcome difficult challenges. Often, they are quests that single characters or small groups of characters could never dream of accomplishing. There can be aspects of puzzles that have to be solved; items that need to be acquired to gain access to the raid area; and finally, there are incredible battles at the center of it all. Raids are also called "end game" content, meant for people who have accomplished everything else in MMORPGs. The term "raid" also can be used in the Player-vs-Player context, where multiple teams of players compete against other teams of players.

Nothing brings a guild (or group) together like difficult combat. Nothing validates a leader more than when he is a part of the combat, leading the battle, fighting with his people. The great guild leaders are fully engaged with what is going on in their guilds, living through the pleasure as well as the pain. The true guild leader serves his people and is one of the people – fighting alongside them in all situations – that's when magic happens on the combat field. That's when people are inspired. When the leader risks his own character alongside others, it gives him more credibility. People will naturally believe in leaders that have combat context. They believe in leaders who have to feel and live with the decisions they make. That is the reason for the fact that the best guild leaders are the ones who have come up through the ranks. People always trust them more. Knowing that your leader has walked in your shoes gives you respect for the person behind the title.

The raid leader (or hunt master) is the person who guides multiple groups of people into battle. He is the one to whom everyone ultimately listens. The best raid leaders do not lose their cool when the battle turns south. If something unexpected happens, they quickly redirect the troops and bring focus back to the task at hand. Raid leaders ensure that strategy is being followed, and they fight side-by-side with the others.

The best raid leaders look for difficult encounters. They want to succeed where others have failed, or where others are stagnating. The leaders always want the difficult tasks, not the easy ones. They want the uncharted territory. They constantly are striving.

Leaders in real life are no different from raid leaders. Leaders serve their people during difficult projects or endeavors. They are fully engaged, working side-by-side with the people living through the good as well as the bad. Leaders guide multiple people or teams of people through challenging situations. The best leaders don't lose their cool when something turns south – instead, they refocus the people as necessary. The best leaders are not looking for the easy projects – they actually seek out the most challenging ones.

Revenues from online games will reach $11.5 billion by 2011.

http://arstechnica.com/news.ars/post/20070912-report-mmorpgs-revenues-to-explode-over-next-few-years.html

Raid Leaders Set Goals, Make Rules & Clarify Tactics

Raid leaders are expected to set goals and communicate whatever strategies are needed to accomplish a successful hunt. If a strategy exists, then the raid leader communicates the ins-and-outs of the strategy – where people should stand, what abilities they can and cannot use, how NPC AI will react, etc. Sometimes, the raid leader needs to do research into strategy. This might require talking to other guilds on the same or other servers, reading forums, scouring YouTube or other websites. If no strategies exist or are known, then it's the best practice for the raid leader to communicate to the rest of the guild involved that they are going in with their own non-battletested strategies. And then, of course, execution of strategy is as important as having the vision in the first place.

Over the years, I have seen some interesting raiding strategies. I've participated in simplistic ones, such as "zerging," which is equivalent to "rush in and kill" or "storming," or strategies of attrition, whereby you would wear down the raid boss (e.g., a dragon or other significant enemy) by continually resurrecting dead people and sending them back into the fray. I've seen innovative strategies whereby class abilities and items were utilized in unusual ways, such as thieves trapping party members with area-of-effect spells in order to kill invisible raid bosses. I've seen elaborate strategies that took months to plan, incorporating spreadsheets, Visio's, etc. Generally, the fewer the people participating in a raid, the greater the need for strategic planning.

If the goal of the raid is to complete a major quest, then there are often prerequisite quests that members need to accomplish. The raid leader ensures that all the requirements for attending and carrying out the event have been met. Raid leaders sometimes will assign functional roles, such as, communication moderators (to monitor and control the communication), item leaders (to hold resources necessary for the quest), treasure leaders (to pick up any resources that are obtained for later distribution), history recorders (taking videos, screenshots), etc. Each person will have a specific responsibility, and each will understand the overarching goals and his own goals.

Raid leaders often set certain ground rules and guidelines to be followed (the initial creation of these rules is usually collaborative). For example, if you have to go AFK (away from keyboard; i.e., something in real life demands your attention), then you must try to establish when you will be back. If you can't do that, then put yourself on auto-follow mode (so that you will follow others into combat), or logout or you may be replaced. A guideline might be that long raids (that last up to 8 hours) will be done only on weekends, and that every hour, a 10 minute break will be allowed. Showing up at a specific time might be a guideline for a raid, as well as guidelines on what classes might or might not be required for the raid. Communication guidelines might exist (no profanity; no overt rudeness; talking limited to raid leaders during the combat; etc.) There are the expectations, of course, that people understand their roles and game mechanics.

To illustrate what a raid is like, below is an excerpt of what you might hear the raid leader say before it begins:

Raid leader: "Okay, once we start, all DPS to the west, healers east, tanks north. Once the main tank has aggro, use DOTs. Healers stay out of range until he AOE's. Make sure all buffs are up, especially str. Careful of wandering trash – and if you pick up any, don't train anyone. Res if main tank goes down, otherwise stay on heals. If you go OOM, then pull back and med. Try to CC his Pets after you debuff him – if you have to, kite one away. Careful, we are KOS once we get past the city."

To clarify, he starts with saying that all character classes with DPS (damage per second abilities, i.e., mages that can do a lot of damage in a short amount of time) move to the west, the healers move east, and the fighters move north. The main tank is the fighter who starts the battle and tries to keep the monster's (or the opposing player's) attention on himself rather than anyone else (e.g. having aggro) – and once the monster is attacking the main tank, then characters can use DOTs (damage over time abilities). He instructs the casters to cast protective spells (buffs) on appropriate characters – most importantly, the ability to increase someone's strength. He then tells the healers to stay out of the range of the monster until the monster uses his area-of-effect ability (perhaps a dragon's breath, which can hit multiple people in a specific area). He says to be careful of weaker monsters (wandering trash) that are not the specific goal at hand – and if any of them come after you, don't lead those monsters to another player – just deal with them on your own. The healers are told to resurrect (res) the main fighter if he dies – but to focus on healing. He also instructs that if any casters have used up all their magical energy, or mana (e.g. they are OOM, or Out Of Mana), then they should withdraw from battle and meditate to restore it. If possible, he requests that the casters who are able to mind control other monsters into hypnotic submission (CC = crowd control) do so to the main monster's allies to keep them out of the battle – but do this only after the casters have tried using spells to remove all protective spells on the main monster. If the crowd control ability does not work and the allies of the monster come after you, then run them away from the battle and keep running. Finally, be careful, because once they get past a particular city, then everything will attack you at the moment when you are seen.

The above example is a more simplistic set of instructions than normally is given in a challenging raid. Some raids require that diagrams be shared with the raid members in order to show explicitly where to stand, in what sequence key actions have to happen, at what period in time, etc.

Sometimes, the goal of a raid may be simply to learn how the environment could be leveraged or what abilities the raid monsters possess. The goal of the raid might be to acquire the next set of keys which open a locked gate. There might be multiple goals to proceed to the next level of the quest. Perhaps there is a goal to complete the raid in a certain amount of time or finish the hunt with no deaths. Ultimately, it's the raid leader's job to call out what the goals and strategies are to accomplish the raid.

Leaders in the real world need to set goals and communicate whatever strategies and tactics are needed for success. They need to be clear on what rules and guidelines exist – for example, in the business world, it may be necessary to clarify telecommute policies or working-from-home guidelines, etc.

78.6 million wireless subscribers will be playing online games in 2009.

http://www.clickz.com/3403931l

Remain Calm Under Fire

I've been a part of multiple encounters where the raid leader lost his composure as things turned south. Perhaps the boss mob had unexpected powers. Maybe someone dropped his internet connection and left the battle. Perhaps the strategy which worked the last 10 times no longer works due to AI tweaks. Whatever the reason, things did not go as planned.

Without exception, if the raid leader started to panic, those around him would waiver as well. Again, when I say "raid leader" in the context of gaming, simply think "leader" in your own context; instead of "raid," think "project". People sense fear. They see confusion. That fear and confusion spreads quickly. First one, then two, then everyone is affected. Maintaining a calm and focused demeanor, even in tense situations, increases the likelihood of a successful raid. Speaking with authority, but not chastising or screaming, generally signifies a strong raid leader. Screamers are those that start shouting obscenities as they lose control of the situation. The ability to remain calm, when everyone else is nervous, is key to a successful raid leader. Instead of letting communication become strained and confused, the exemplary raid leader focuses his directives to be laser sharp.

Usually, it is the experienced raid leader, the one who understands game mechanics, character nuance, people's personalities, and strategy, that is able to repeatedly deliver. I have found, generally, that if a raid leader can keep his cool under fire, then he has a higher degree of self-control in all situations. He tends to have more patience. Where some people lose their composure during an emergency – the raid leader shines and maintains control.

Inaction is another sign of loss of composure. Analysis paralysis is another. The successful raid leader would prefer to make the call and manage through the results, rather than wait to make a better informed decision. Split-second decision-making is required for the raid leader – and to do this, he needs to be able to filter out the noise in any situation, distill the relevant data, and then quickly do what is needed on the battle field. There exists no luxury of time or consensus in raids –

disciplined decisions need to be made constantly, without being fully informed.

Remaining calm under fire applies to all situations, not just combat. It is a trait that is needed when meeting with others, when receiving criticism, in emails and on the phone. In general, all communication benefits from having a level head. It's the mature leader who has learned the importance of maintaining composure in all situations, in both the real and virtual worlds.

While many parents don't play video games with their children, some have had positive experiences. "(Halo 3) has bonded me with him," said Marvin Paup, 33, of Golden Valley, Ariz of his 10-year-old son Allen. "It's like a whole new reality with me and him."

http://ap.google.com/article/ALeqM5if3tJjIxhz596nF_zjpcPWstHt5gD8SSC7HO2

Have a Backup Plan

Sometimes raids do not go as planned or hoped. It isn't uncommon for "wipes" to occur, where every single member of the raid (this can be over fifty people) dies. The greater the significance of the battle (or loss potential), the more planning and backup scenarios are needed.

In one online game that I played, the worst setback you could suffer was an "eat." This is when your character was literally eaten by the creature that he was fighting. An eat could set you back months of hard-core playing – some players have played for years and not reached level 50. Potentially, you could lose gear permanently in certain situations. One of the most dangerous eaters was the mother of all dragons, (a.k.a., "Mama"). The name wrought fear in people for years. Early on, guilds would try Mama at partial power, perhaps not fully protected or not wearing the proper gear, and they would sometimes die and get eaten in mass numbers. This often would destroy the morale of some players and they would quit the game. My guild chose to plan. We tested different strategies and techniques. We kept testing until we were confident that we could do it. We went in and were the first guild to kill her legitimately and with no deaths – relying on multiple backup plans and strategies mid-fight.

Sometimes, strategies that once worked are rendered ineffective due to changes by the developers – they might add new abilities to the monsters or update their AI to behave differently. The prepared guilds either think on the fly or have developed backup plans. They have key procedures which they execute when certain crises hit – for example, they might have a pre-established fallback leader, so that if the raid leader dies (or becomes disconnected from the chat channels), then everyone knows who will call the shots. Identifying alternative communication mechanisms can be important. Another backup plan might be to utilize established combat techniques that worked in other areas of the game – for example, use fire-based spells in an icy environment.

In real life, having backup plans and mitigation strategies are integral to success. If option A doesn't succeed, be prepared to quickly go to option B. The more important or significant the endeavor, the greater emphasis needs to exist on having a backup plan.

Regardless of the outcome, let the team figure out what worked well and what could have been better. Add in your insight, as well. Sometimes you don't succeed in spite of planning. When that happens, good leaders accept blame and responsibility. They forgive others and themselves. They realize that mistakes and problems happen. The good leaders learn from their mistakes and don't repeat them. They take their licks and move on.

Anshe Chung was the first Second Life entrepreneur to earn more than $1,000,000 in virtual in-game real estate development and design.

http://www.msnbc.msn.com/id/22574057/page/3/

Some Risks are Good

To be successful in raids, risk is often necessary and encouraged. I've had significant success, in my online gaming life, against risks that others weren't comfortable taking. Whenever I was trying to accomplish something, I would always evaluate multiple strategies to achieve my goal; I weighed the risks versus the rewards; I created plans and implemented them, and then I continuously strove to improve upon my methods. Ultimately, I tried to mitigate the risk as much as possible. I liked doing things before anyone else, so that much of what I did was risk-oriented. I was always open to failure, and I couldn't handle being too scared to try. Identifying "outside-the-box" (but legal) strategies for accomplishing anything is a very rewarding activity to me.

Being the first person to set foot in a new area is exciting, and dangerous, from an MMORPG perspective. New monsters with unknown abilities require you to be able to create strategies on the fly; new puzzles with deadly traps lurk around every corner; both death and rewards abound for the brave. Going down in history as having been the first is also enticing to some. With any new significant endeavor comes the realization that risk is good and needed.

There are a variety of risks in online games. There can be risks to your character in the game, in terms of item loss, attribute loss, or prestige loss, and so on. There are, also, risks that affect people's real lives due their inability to exercise good judgment in terms of hours spent online -- personal relationships or one's job can suffer. In addition, there are real financial risks that some people are willing to take, spending thousands of dollars on virtual items, currency, and characters.

I have had some discussions with non-gamers and lax-gamers regarding their idea that there are no "true" risks in online games. I can understand and appreciate that perspective. However, I must reiterate here that some gamers take the risks into the real world because of their gaming addictions. They risk their relationships with their families. They risk their jobs. They risk, in my opinion, too much. There is huge risk in excessive investment of time – and time can be more valuable than money. Therefore, I believe that there are, for those who don't practice self-control, real and serious life-changing risks associated with online gaming.

> **From October 2006 to October 2007, $1 billion was invested in virtual-world companies.**
>
> http://www.marketingvox.com/archives/2007/10/09/1-billion-invested-in-35-virtual-world-companies-in-past-12-months/

Jump First

Along with taking risks, raid leaders should jump first. They should be spearheading the charge against the unknown. They should be pushing the envelope on the quests that people think are not possible. "Can't" should not be in the vocabulary of the raid leader – it is too paralyzing. Some raid leaders are not willing to take calculated risks – so they lose out on a special kind of learning that comes only with taking risks. Jump first does not necessarily mean that the raid leader is literally the first to engage the raid monster in battle, nor does it preclude that. It does mean that they are pushing the limit, as a group, to be first.

Leaders need to be willing to take risks in the real world as well. In my opinion, it is often better to make a decision and manage through it than make no decision in fear that it is the wrong one. Leaders need to be risk-tolerant.

There is significant ambiguity and uncertainty that comes with doing a raid for the first time. Some raid leaders have doubts about whether they will be able to influence the direction properly. Performance anxiety can occur as well. Some are concerned that they will be judged based on their ability to lead a guild to success. All of these are limiting or constraining factors that the effective raid leader disregards.

Along the lines of jumping first is leading by example. Great leaders know that they should be modeling the behavior that they expect from their people. They don't wait for solutions - they create them. They don't just tell people where to go - they lead them there. They create the appropriate standards of excellence and then set the example for others to follow. Ultimately, they run towards the train wreck to help; they don't wait for others to come to them; they walk the talk and lean into the wind.

Raids are analogous to projects in real life. If there is a project with pain, that looks daunting, take it head on. Tackle it with fervor. Drive the solution. Know you can do it. Take it one step at a time. Lead your people through the battle to glory.

Loot Distribution

In some online games, the acquisition of wealth and items can be a large motivator for gamers. Recognition and achievement are often high on the totem pole – growing one's character is a central premise in almost all MMORPGs. Interpersonal relationships are also a key motivator for certain players. In all situations which allow some sort of reward distribution, i.e., those that occur at the end of successful raids, a method must be created in order to best reward and motivate the troops.

There is no salary in online games (well, there are people who are paid to play). Some guilds require their players to pay a recurring tithe into guild coffers. These guilds are generally comprised of people who put the goals of the whole over the goals of the individual. They are not loose bands of people who half-heartedly come together in name only for purely social reasons. They are a tight family working together, rowing in the same direction.

The closest parallel to salary would be the distribution of items from raids and quests, activities that require many people working together towards a common goal, usually resulting in the attainment of such items and wealth. Guilds distribute the loot to their members in a variety of ways. When members stop participating in guild activities, they generally are kicked out.

The tightest guilds, those where trust runs high, have members who are willing to risk their necks without requiring knowledge of how they will be rewarded. Sometimes the nature of the rewards is not even known. Sometimes the mechanism by which the rewards will be distributed is not known. There is enough trust in the guild and in raid leaders to do the right thing, such that in the long run, everyone will be fairly compensated for their actions. Ultimately, there is trust in the guild leader to reward based either on merit or on his perception of what makes the guild the strongest.

Some guilds have their members roll virtual dice randomly as a loot distribution mechanism. This can bring a fun gambling aspect into the game, but it can lead, also, to dissatisfied "unlucky" players – this is reward based on luck rather than performance, and a common reward distribution mechanism for impromptu groups of players that form in order to accomplish a particular goal (guilded and non-guilded), where there is insufficient trust or history established to do it in any other way. However, the practice of rewarding those who have worked the hardest or the longest will lead to a stronger guild.

Dragon Kill Points, or DKPs, are another system by which loot distribution occurs. Dragons are historically one of the most challenging creatures to destroy in an MMORPG. Killing a dragon might require 50+ people working collaboratively for many contiguous hours. Unfortunately, only 3 or 4 items may be the reward for killing that dragon – so, many players would get no reward, other than recognition and a sense of achievement. In 1999, a player named Thott, in a guild called "Afterlife" (a competitor to my guild, "Fires of Heaven," in Everquest), created the concept of DKPs. This is a point-based system where players receive points for attending guild events. The number of points that a guild member has accumulated determines his relative ability to acquire items from guild events, since these points can then be used to bid for or buy items, based on their point values, which are either predetermined (by the game itself) or established by the guild leader.

Some online games give their players tools to track DKPs internally in the game. A DKP system might factor in how long a player spends at an activity and award points accordingly. Also, guild leaders might award points to players for doing certain mundane tasks (such as farming or mining or other activities that few people seem to enjoy) – as an incentive, since these tasks lead to achievements toward more grandiose goals.

The main problem with many DKP systems is that they don't reward based on performance. Instead, they reward based on attendance. The more you attend, the more points you get. I have never agreed with that method of loot distribution, but I acknowledge that it makes decisions easy and the system is simple to manage. I think that there is no 100% "fair" system. However, as every raid leader comes to realize, significant effort must be put into establishing mechanisms and guidelines for loot distribution.

Approximately .15% of the world's population plays World of Warcraft.
(over 10 million subscriptions).

http://www.blizzard.com/press/

Give Your People the Best Loot

Raid leaders realize that you need to give your people the best loot (i.e., rewards). This realization comes with experience. When I first started playing online games, I was greedy. If I found something good, I wanted it. If I was part of a guild, I hoped that I, rather than anyone else, would get the powerful items. Even if it didn't directly benefit me, I still wanted it because I could sell it. I always wanted more. The focus was on me.

As I matured, my focus switched from putting myself first to putting the guild first. If I found something good, I gave it to whomever could best utilize it. The whole became stronger. As I moved up the ranks, I continued to shift my focus further towards serving others. The more I did this, the stronger the group became. I didn't neglect myself; I simply didn't put my needs over the needs of the whole.

The more I shifted to being externally focused, the more I was inwardly rewarded. If we succeeded on a difficult raid encounter, it gave me great joy to let my teammates take the best loot. I often would give out my share of the loot to others as well, unless they insisted that I keep it. Over time, I noticed that others began to take the same stance. We were more interested in the collective whole becoming stronger, rather than in the individual. We wanted the entire guild to succeed, not just a few select members of it.

As I previously mentioned, a great programmer could be 5x (at least) as effective as an average one. Yet, often, they are rewarded only incrementally more. I've always felt that people should be rewarded exactly what they are worth, not more, not less. Eventually you will lose that great programmer if you don't reward him appropriately. If someone is worth more, fight for him (or her). If the structure doesn't allow for more, then fight to change the structure.

Giving your people the best loot means striving to reward others before yourself; it means giving them the perks for which you might be eligible; it ultimately means putting others before yourself. Take care of your people. Give them the best loot and continue on your path to become a successful leader.

Eve Online, an MMOG, has commissioned a dedicated real world economist to perform ongoing analysis of economic indicators, such as inflation, economic growth and price trends in the game.

http://www.virtualworldsnews.com/money/index.html

Give Constant Feedback and Appropriate Recognition

More important than loot can be simply telling the raiders how they performed, regardless of the outcome -- and the more specific, the better. Telling your healers how well they kept people alive when a battle was difficult is important; or, what a great job your thief did in disarming the traps to get to the raid; clapping your warriors on their backs for maintaining aggro (i.e., keeping the monster targeting them rather than "squishy" mages) or applauding the sorcerers who unloaded incredible amounts of damage. Give your people credit and acknowledgment. It's an easy thing to do, yet it is so often overlooked. "Props," or giving people respect, can motivate more than material gain.

During and after a hunt (small or large scale), it is common for leaders to give feedback on performance. This is a normal behavior in MMORPGs; there is generally no excessive praise (you can find overly harsh critics in immature leaders). Feedback comes, also, from other players in the environment. The online gaming environment is conducive to constant feedback, and there is a lot of opportunity for recognition. This feedback can come from direct personalized chats, from open chats, from in-game public channels, on forums, in emails, over voice, and so on.

Feedback and recognition obviously go beyond raiding into any activity: if a guild mate is doing a great job collecting resources or helping others; if people are striving to keep negative conflict at bay; if someone accomplishes something in real-life, such as, getting married, graduating from school, receiving a promotion, etc. It is integral for people to understand that they are contributing toward goals of the guild and that they matter (speaking of getting married – as a healer character, I've been asked and have performed quite a few virtual marriages in various online games). This happens constantly in the online world. Unlike the real world, I've never partaken in "annual reviews" of my officers or guild mates. There is no need. They always know where they stand, as feedback is continuous. The environment contributes to that.

Real world leaders should strive to give feedback on performance as much as possible. Recognize what went well on a project or endeavor and identify areas for improvement.

Giving constant feedback is a fast and effective way to bring vision and goals always into perspective. People's expectations can be continually nudged in the right direction. Morale, and thus, retention of people, increases with a positive stream of feedback. Recognition for risk-taking encourages further risk-taking. Always incent and validate the behavior you seek. Feedback is helpful for everyone, as it is a way to make everyone's capabilities known, giving praise and credit where it is due.

People thrive on recognition. Effective leaders always spend the few moments it takes to acknowledge a job well done. It behooves leaders to seize all opportunities to recognize excellence. Of course, many times, even actions less than excellent deserve recognition. One must be thoughtful regarding this issue.

Summary

- Nothing brings a guild or team together like a difficult combat or other extreme situation/project. Growth comes through striving to win, not necessarily from the outcome.

- Leaders should put their own butts on the line, alongside everyone in their guild.

- The best raid leaders come up through the ranks of the guild.

- Leaders are expected to set goals and communicate whatever strategies are needed to be successful.

- Leaders often set certain ground rules and guidelines to be followed.

- The most effective leaders maintain a high degree of self-control in all situations.

- Leaders have multiple backup plans.

- Leaders look for difficult challenges, not easy ones.

- Regardless of the outcome, let the team figure out what worked well and what could have been better.

- Risk-taking should be encouraged, motivated, incented, and rewarded.

- Leaders should jump first – and lead by example.

- The best leaders give their people the best loot.

- Give constant feedback on people's performance. Morale and retention increase with a positive stream of feedback.

- Incent and validate the behavior you seek.

- In any endeavor, execution of strategy is as important as the vision itself.

- Feedback is a fast and effective way to bring the vision and goals into focus.

CHAPTER 5: METRICS

How can leaders effectively utilize metrics? Can a leader manage what he can't measure? What are effective metrics? In this chapter, I hope to answer these and other pertinent questions.

Metrics in Online Games

Metrics are simply a standardized way to assess performance. They are a tool that certain guild leaders utilize to assess a guild's ability to meet various guild objectives. Metrics that guild leaders could utilize include: wealth (at the guild or individual level); market share of items found on server or world; market share of areas discovered; etc. Adding more granularities to the metric can make it more useful, such as wealth gained per week, or sales per item type, or even sales per item type per week per character. The more useful the metric, the better the decision-making becomes. The more you can predict the results of whatever your guild is trying to accomplish, the less risk and the greater the opportunity for success. If metrics are trending in the wrong direction, then rectifying action needs to be taken. For example, if your guild wealth, relative to other guilds, is falling on the scoreboards, then something needs to change. Many guilds do not utilize or care about scoreboards or how their characters are performing – but some do.

There are lots of interesting metrics that some online game servers provide: class and race breakdown among all players, percentage of characters within certain level ranges, total kills, NPC discoveries, total deaths, quests completed, kill versus death ratio, missions completed, items crafted, work order success ratio, and a variety of other statistics. Information can be sliced and diced within a single server or over all servers, and sometimes even between American and European players. You can also find metrics on time played. For example, number of hours played this week or to date. In some online games, people have over 100 days played (that's greater than 2,400 hours played).

I love stats. Demographics. Records. Statistics have always fascinated me. I used to maintain elaborate spreadsheets of character data trending over time to assess performance of my characters (as well as others) in online games. It was fun pouring through reams of data to try to identify ways to continuously improve. I would jot down how long it took us to finish a hunt with a new strategy. I had accurate records on how long it took us to gather resources needed for specific quests.

Since our guild vision was often to become the most dominant guild in the game, the metrics and scorecards that I cared about measured things such as our characters' accomplishments and abilities relative to others. If we moved down on the global scoreboard scorecard, we knew that others were playing more hours and/or more efficiently. We not only watched our movement on the lists, but we watched others to see how everyone was trending. If suddenly someone popped onto the board out of nowhere, then they were potentially cheating (which sometimes happens in games) – and perhaps they should be reported to the administrators (and if they suddenly disappeared off the charts, they were most likely deleted or banned).

Key Performance Indicators (KPIs) are just metrics that are tied to a target goal. For example, if our goal was to sell 5 platinum worth of gems every week, then the KPI would represent how much above or below our target we were that week (e.g., we are at -1 plat per week). I never got to the point of implementing formal KPIs – but we did have general weekly/monthly/etc. goals and would talk about how we were trending and how close we were to our goals. Again, while this might sound too bureaucratic or process-heavy, we implemented things as simply as possible. In this case, the hardcore players had weekly goals for how many experience levels they wanted to gain or how much product they wanted to sell, etc.

The simplistic metrics which we utilized in my guild made people feel more accountable for their commitments. People felt compelled when everyone's goals were transparent, and they had a clear sense of achievement when they reached their targets. We tended to utilize in-game scorecards and dashboards rather than to create our own – although occasionally we would. I didn't always share with everyone the metrics that I kept. I didn't want to remove the "game" aspect and make people feel obligated to perform at a certain level (though everyone had high expectations of one another) – I kept track of things more for my own understanding and interest in statistical data. Whenever the game began to feel like a job was when I would re-evaluate what was going on – and I would try to bring back the fun.

We also watched how others were progressing on existing standardized metrics – for example, if another guild was trending faster in an area that we were competing in, it would potentially change how we operated. Should we focus our efforts more? Should we merge with another guild? Acquire another guild? Become more efficient in what we were doing? Add more members? It was a great way to see how we performed relative to other guilds. We also would exert more energy on going to those individuals or guilds in the game to understand what they were doing that was yielding the results that they had. We would evaluate what they were doing and then incorporate and improve on their strategies as possible.

Understanding how game-wide metrics are calculated (what makes them go up or down) also was to be leveraged if our goal was merely to go higher on the lists. Watching the metrics allowed us to set aggressive goals in areas where we were not leading. It also made us newly aware of such areas, so that we could begin to make changes. Again, I was always cognizant of keeping the game fun – but I did notice that the more people watched a known metric, the more self-regulation and performance improvements occurred.

Some of the metrics that I kept were useful in forecasting sales based on how our crafters were selling. Seeing fluctuations in drop rates for specific items made us strive to acquire different resources after each game-server software patch/upgrade (Often times, developers will tweak the chances that certain resources will randomly show up – and when they tweak things positively, it's good to capitalize on that and act quickly before they are tweaked back down). Watching metrics on market trends allowed us to capitalize on changing market conditions quickly and effectively. We watched the trends in terms of what was selling and for how much in order to optimize the purchasing or selling of certain resources. For example, in one game, we had the market on a specific rare gem – we had found a particular location where the drop rate was high, relative to all other gems. We farmed that specific resource day and night until we had tons of the gem – then we slowly fed the market. Being able to watch who was selling what and in what quantity allowed us to identify successfully performing harvesters – who then became candidates for us to watch to learn how and where they were playing.

Another useful metric which I tracked concerned loot distribution. For example: how long an individual was waiting to get an item that he wanted; what people were getting the most or least items; how well we were equipping everyone in our guild based on what they wanted or needed. It was interesting for me to compare my observations over different areas or times.

Accurate metrics also let me plan certain raids and quests as I charted people's growth performance rates – I could then forecast when we would be able to accomplish various challenges, based on our current growth projections. This planning process let me optimize the timing, so that when the day hit, we were ready to execute (rather than waste time doing other things). We wanted to do things first, and we needed to ensure that everything was in place on the right day and at the right time for all characters in our guild, so that all we had to do was execute.

There are metrics in MMORPGs that track your computer's performance, like FPS (frames-per-second), which tell you how fast your computer's graphics card is performing. If you see less than 10 FPS, then your card is barely able to play the game. You can start lagging (think of a stuttering car engine), so that the game play is no longer smooth. This can be an indication that you should lower your graphics settings or try a variety of other things to improve performance. Lag leads to death. If your FPS is 30 or higher, you can feel assured that game play will be smooth. Another metric that people watch is ping times, which represent network performance. This, again, is useful to track because if your network connections are not good, it is best not to try difficult quests. The number of concurrent players online is another metric that can be utilized in decision-making. If there are too many people online, or if too many are in the area in which you plan to adventure, it is possible that the game servers or your computer server will be unable to adequately perform.

Some games offer "healing meters" and "damage-per-second meters," which are mechanisms by which some aspects of performance are measured. Some people strive to always be on top of those lists, as indication of how well they are performing their roles. As with any metric that is followed blindly, being on the top isn't always an indication of being the "best." For example – there are some practices that help you move higher on the healing meter list, but at the expense of the party – a player might not cast defensive spells in order to encourage their party members to take more damage (so that they can heal more) – or they might significantly increase downtime (time between battles) because they are not managing their mana appropriately in order to move up on the healing charts – plus they might be wasting guild resources (such as mana potions) because of the short-sightedness of their playing style. Some guilds even go as far as kicking people out of their guild if they are not performing well based on those metrics. However, the exemplary guilds take a lot more into account rather than being blindly led by the metric – they also factor in a lot of other intangibles, such as mana management, buffs, dispelling, and a variety of other considerations before making a decision to kick out a member. Utilize the metric but don't be a slave to it.

Bottom line, effective leaders are constantly assessing themselves and are trying to improve in all aspects of what they do. Metrics are a useful tool for some aspects of assessment and improvement, and they help in the many facets of decision-making and planning. Many people don't formally use them, and some utilize them without even realizing it.

It generally takes an average person about 600 hours to reach the highest level (currently 70th level) possible in World of Warcraft.

http://news.bbc.co.uk/2/hi/technology/7007026.stm

Operational Dashboards and Reports

In the online world, we live and die (literally) by our operational dashboards and reports. Dashboards are focused on tactical operational data instead of strategic goals. Information, such as how much health a character has, is represented in a graphical format for easy consumption. In this way, if you are in a group of forty people, you can visually assess everyone's health. When health goes to zero, you are dead, so it is a vital metric to keep tabs on. You also see colored information which represents one's state – for example, a green health bar might indicate that a character is poisoned and is in need of curing. Also, there is information on how much mana (or magical energy) your guild mates have, how much endurance they have, etc. There are dashboards that represent what classes are within a certain distance from you (for example, how many healers are within shouting distance and could come to lend a helping hand); what people's experience levels are, which is an indication of performance; dashboards which indicate if people are looking to join a group (useful in creating pick-up-groups for questing) or if guilds are recruiting new members, and a variety of other dashboards. Each online game has its own variants of dashboards. This information can improve forecasting and planning for any activity, and it improves your ability to take calculated risks.

There are, also, game dashboards that show listings of wealth, which character and guild has found the most areas or has crafted the most items, etc. Dashboards show, for example, what guilds have killed the most monsters and what guilds have discovered the most unique items. In addition, there are dashboards which trend population growth on servers, wealth acquired over time, and much more.

Dashboards are utilized heavily in raiding -- dashboards that show player health, player magic, player endurance, and a variety of other easy-to-consume metrics which facilitate quick and relevant decision-making. Without accurate dashboards with this operational information, it would be significantly more difficult to be successful in raids or in general questing. Communication would have to operate at an entirely new level to compensate for the lack of operational dashboards.

Ask yourself how dashboards could be better leveraged in the real world. Can you easily communicate people's skillsets? Workloads? Vacation schedules? Project status? Project accomplishments?

Sometimes You Have to Manage What You Can't Measure

"You can't manage what you can't measure." That sounds defeatist to me. I think that people need to realize that they sometimes have to manage what they don't (or can't) measure. You might not be able to measure a guild-mate's trust in you, or measure why teenage audiences see their cell phones as a fashion accessory, or measure why a customer acts irrationally or illogically, but you still need to manage through it. Can you measure your love of your spouse or your child (people would retort that you can't manage love)? Can you measure someone's humility? Can you measure your integrity? Can you measure your marketing department? Your lawyers that you keep on retainer? Even if you can't come up with a useful metric, you still need to manage through it.

Much of what leaders do revolves around strategic decision-making, where facts simply don't exist yet or cannot be measured. For example, the rules that govern the online game world change on the whim of the designers and developers. Waiting for facts might leave you behind the competition. That doesn't mean that you jump to decisions without any facts – it does mean that you maintain a balance and don't accept the negative adage, "you can't manage what you don't (or can't) measure."

Measuring is often about metrics, but some metrics can miss the mark. For example, measurements such as "number of bugs per thousand lines of code" can lead to the wrong sorts of coding practices -- poorly optimized, bloated code. Yes, more code will be generated, but what is the quality of that code? How about this metric: "number of calls by a customer service rep in a day" -- this generally accomplishes the intended goal of increasing the CSR's throughput. It also often has the unintended result of CSRs who rush through their calls, giving poor customer service.

Leveraging a metric as part of your decision-making process makes sense when it is a good metric. The metric needs to be contextually understood and needs to have been created with thought. Leaders know that any metrics that they utilize need to be effective.

Entropia, a massively multiplayer online universe, had a virtual item (an asteroid space resort) sold for $100,000.

http://www.marketwire.com/mw/release.do?id=770780

Create Effective Metrics

Putting metrics in place will affect behavior. Heisenberg's uncertainty principle tells you that you can't measure something in a system without affecting the system. There was an experiment in the early 1900's to understand how lighting conditions affected productivity (at a factory called "Hawthorne Works"). The researchers found that if they increased illumination, productivity increased!

They increased lighting levels again -- and, voilà, productivity increased again! It seemed too good to be true. They decided to lower lighting conditions to levels before the start of their research. Once again, productivity increased... They came to the conclusion that it had little to do with lighting and more to do with the fact that workers' productivity went up when they realized that a bunch of scientists were closely monitoring them, scribbling furiously as they worked. This became known as the "Hawthorne Effect" (where people's behavior and performance change if observed).

In order to make an effective metric, it is important to be cognizant of what behavior could result from implementing a new metric -- you don't want one person to "hit his targets" at the expense of the whole team. For example – you might be tracking how much wealth each person is gaining, which, in turn, reflects the guild's collective wealth. However, if one individual is selling a resource (let's say potions of invisibility) that is needed by the entire guild for an important raid, then you might need to holistically re-evaluate the relative priorities of goals and look deeper into what sorts of behaviors your goals and metrics are creating.

The majority of guild leaders exert very little effort in collecting or creating metrics. Most simply leverage subsets of metrics which the game environments provide. If they do create a metric, they know to keep it simple. A good rule of thumb might be: if your grandmother who doesn't play MMORPGs understands the metric, then everyone will. It is important to avoid spending too much overhead on collecting metrics – there is no such thing as a perfect metric, but there are such things as detrimental ones. It is also key to focus on the quality of a metric over the quantity. More metrics can mean simply more waste. If certain metrics are not being utilized as part of the decision-making process, then those metrics should not exist. The value of metrics can change over time, so that they should be evaluated on some sort of basis. For example, once all my guild members reached max character level, there was no more point in tracking their growth performance. It is also important to make sure that there is no disconnect between management and the troops – if people on the ground know that the metric is garbage, but management is looking at it as gospel, there is a big disconnect. Perception can hurt more than reality. Garbage in, garbage out.

If good metrics can be created, published, and tracked for all to view, they can provide an easy way for members to understand how they are contributing to team goals. This allows self-management as well as mechanisms for others to help out those who might be lagging behind – and it provides visibility of the outlying performers, which then might inspire others to observe, evaluate, adopt, and then improve. For example: if a guild's goal is to grow its membership, then the number of guild-mates over the dimension of time is a useful metric. Sharing this metric on internal guild forums and over chat channels can emphasize the goal and turn that goal into a game within a game. Who can recruit the most new members this month? People will put greater emphasis on recruiting. The guild may reward recruits based on who brought them to the table. Granted, quality of recruit may suffer.

The more people that exist in the guild, the more metrics tend to be leveraged. The key to metrics in online games is for guild leaders to acquire whatever data is needed to help them understand and improve the state and performance of their guild.

The same is true in the real world. For more informed decision-making, it is integral for leaders to be able to quickly understand the state and performance of their business (etc.).

Islands of Kesmai, an ASCII based MORPG, released by CompuServe in 1984, charged $12/hour to play.

http://www.tharsis-gate.org/articles/imaginary/HISTOR~1.HTM

Adopt a Strategy-Based People Management Philosophy

While I believe that metrics are a great tool for decision-making, you have to be careful not to take it too far. Too broad a decision should not be made based solely on a metric – leverage the metric for simple decisions, and look to them to identify areas that need deeper analysis, but never make significant decisions purely because of the metric. One mistake that I once made was from watching character scoreboard metrics. The top players in the game were represented on the scoreboard. It was always the same dozen or so players that held the top ten spots for a long time. One day, a new player popped into the top spot out of nowhere – something we had seen only once before, when a player had cheated. I assumed that this person also had cheated, and I called his integrity into question. I was wrong. I learned that the developer had changed the way in which the scoreboard metric was calculated, changing only one of the top ten players (and bringing a new person into the top ten). You need not only to understand exactly how the metric is created, but, also, you need to look deeply into and beyond the metrics.

A few quality measures related to achieving guild vision are much more valuable than a bunch of mediocre measures. So, if becoming the wealthiest guild in the game is the goal of the guild, then measures such as each character's wealth gained per week are good; overall guild gains are good; other characters' wealth gains should be monitored; how often characters are selling items (which ties directly to wealth) is good, etc. It is important to factor in all of your metrics to get a partial view of how well you are performing on your strategic vision – and accept that you won't have a truly holistic representation of your organization. That comes with looking beyond the metrics and into the nuances of the people, your competitors, etc. Metrics often measure tactical aspects of the guild – so one must guard against using tactical metrics in place of strategy to guide the guild.

Instead of adopting a "metrics-based management" philosophy, I would advocate for a "strategy-based people management" philosophy, which puts the focus on strategy and people but still leverages metrics as a tool in decision-making. Using the word "metrics," when you are speaking of a management style, takes the emphasis and the collective conscience away from strategy, which is where the focus should be. The metrics which you do create should tie into where you want to take your guild. Your management style (or philosophy) will invariably draw, in part, on your collective life experiences as well as current observations, factoring in metrics – which is good. The focus always should be on strategy, even if your metrics are aligned with measuring your achievement of strategy.

Summary

- Metrics are simply a standardized way to assess performance. They are a tool that certain leaders utilize to measure a guild's (or business's, or team's, etc.) ability to meet various guild objectives.

- If metrics are trending in the wrong direction, then rectifying action needs to be taken.

- Key Performance Indicators (KPIs) are just metrics that are tied to a target goal.

- Metrics are a useful tool for some aspects of assessment and improvement, and they help in many facets of decision-making and planning.

- In the online world, people live and die (literally) by data from operational dashboards.

- Sometimes you have to manage what you can't measure.

- The process itself of putting metrics in place will affect behavior.

- Adopt a strategy-based people management philosophy -- put the focus on strategy but still leverage metrics as a tool in decision-making.

CHAPTER 6: STRATEGY

What is the importance of strategy to a leader? What sorts of strategies are there? What are the implications and outcomes of utilizing certain strategies? This segment seeks to provide answers to these and other strategy-related questions.

MMORPG Strategies

If vision is the goal, strategy is the method or series of plans to attain the goal. The word "strategy" comes from the Greek word "stratÄgos," which is derived from two words: stratos (army) and ago (ancient Greek for leading). Strategy is everything in online games. Strategy is involved in raiding, questing, recruiting, retention, marketing, communicating, relations, resource acquisition and consumption, mergers and acquisitions, selling, vision, leading, building characters, etc.

Serious MMORPG players develop plans for how they want their characters to grow, and all of their actions align with their strategy, from choosing professions to acquiring equipment to gaining stats. As players transition from "casual" to "hard-core" (serious), they often similarly transition from tactical to strategic. Many players start out casual – they jump into a game, quickly pick a class, and start exploring the world. After they have gained a few levels and developed a feel for the game, they often start over (perhaps because the class they originally picked isn't performing as well as they would like, or because they were impressed with the abilities of another character, or because they simply like variety). Generally, players will grow their second character faster than their first – they won't make the same mistakes; they plan a bit more for their future. Whether they start over or not, players begin to take a longer term perspective as they come to appreciate the time commitment that games require. With experience comes strategy.

Guilds and companies often follow the same path as players. They start out tactical, and then, if they persist, they slowly transition to strategic. Guilds and companies without strategy will remain static or are chaotic in nature, while those that take a long term view tend to prosper. In spite of the importance of strategy, major decisions frequently are made without ample consideration of strategic concerns. My belief that strategy is king and that one must always play for the future is what enticed me to work as an enterprise architect in my real life – where our mantra is that today's solutions need to enable tomorrow's business (or, our goal is that the solutions of today must not become the problems of tomorrow).

Strategies always should provide tangible results. Time should not be wasted on strategy that does not deliver a desired outcome. A "virtual" strategy is useless if it is not implementable – of course, sometimes the only way to find out is to try. Having a strategy is often what separates those who deliver from those who do not.

Strategies often are adaptable. They act more as compasses to follow when executing rather than as rigid recipes that require strict adherence. If a strategy is general, there is a greater likelihood that it can be leveraged in multiple situations. For example, high-level raid strategies might include a precedence for healing (self first, then the tank, then others, etc.) or a priority of targets (identify and target the most damaging monsters first or last; go after closest targets first; etc.) The more specific the strategy, the less it can be reused.

The life cycle of strategic planning consists of having a vision of what needs to be accomplished; identifying obstacles to achieving that vision; identifying solutions to those problems; and, finally, communication. For example: a guild might need a strategy for acquiring healing herbs as part of the greater strategy of controlling resources that heal members on raids. The obstacles to acquiring herbs might be the fact that there are few high-level players who are willing to harvest herbs in difficult areas, or that a competing guild is purchasing all the needed resources. The solutions could entail recruiting new players with the needed skills or asking existing players to learn new skills (or infinite other possibilities). It is better to ask the guild members to come up with solutions to the problems (than do it in a vacuum), so that more people have buy-in – and asking also serves as an opportunity to communicate when the guild needs to accomplish something.

If a guild (or person or company) sells resources to others, they need to ask themselves what differentiates them from their competitors. If the supplier guild (or person or company) disappeared over night, and their customers were hardly impacted (because they could get their supplies elsewhere at a similar price or service), then the supplier had best rethink his strategies. How do you become entwined in the lives of your consumers? That's where strategy comes in. If you can disappear, and there is almost no impact, then you really haven't differentiated yourself enough.

"IGE, the largest online seller of virtual goods in the United States, has set up an office in Shanghai to collect virtual currency and assets from more than 1,000 Chinese suppliers and sell them to American players at fat prices."

http://mmopub.com/2007/07/07/still-more-news-on-chinese-gold-farmers/

Combat Principles

Strategy and tactics are closely related – strategy is large scale and tactics are small scale. Carl von Clausewitz, one of the most famous strategic theorists, defined military strategy as "the employment of battles to gain the end of war." Sun Tzu (actual name was Sun Wu) was an influential Chinese military strategist who said "Do not repeat the tactics which have gained you one victory, but let your methods be regulated by the infinite variety of circumstances." He articulated 13 principles of warfare in his famous book, "Art of War." Napoleon had 115 military maxims. The US Army has 9 principles of combat strategy, for which I will draw parallels to online gaming and difficult business situations or projects:

Objective – make sure that everyone understands and is focused on achieving the clearly defined goal. In MMORPG combat, this goal generally revolves around the destruction of a monster. Every operation (battle) should contribute to achieving the strategic goal of the war (raid). In any business endeavor, it is important that everyone understands precisely what they are trying to accomplish and how their actions contributes to (or hinders) the various business goals.

Offensive – seize, retain, and exploit the initiative. At the root of all successful combat is going on the offensive. Defensive playing in MMORPGs is generally useful only in situations demanding retreat (or in operations that demand holding a position). In business, offensive means being first, remaining on top of the competitors, and never losing momentum. It is also about constantly having drive/initiative.

Mass – focus combat power at a specific place and time. In MMORPGs, group leaders put the strength of their attacking forces on the boss (or raid monster) itself, rather than its weaker allies. Strategies need to exist where certain types of force might be preferential at certain points in time (for example, if a dragon is fighting from above, bows might be more effective than certain spells; or ice-based damage might be the preferred strategy, etc.) "Mass" also can be about expelling all energy in the shortest burst of time possible, rather than attempting to hold back any reserves. An example would be casters using spells that cost three times the mana for only fifty percent more damage. The damage-to-mana ratio might not be the best, but it might be necessary in certain situations. Mass in business pertains to focusing people and resources in specific areas at specific times. For example, pulling people from one project to help on a higher priority one or motivating people to work longer for a period of time to get the job done.

Economy of Force – distribute forces wisely so that less-powerful creatures are dealt with as minimally as possible. For example, raid creatures often have weaker allies, but they still need some attention or they can overwhelm the party. In business, this is about being prudent with where and how your people spend their time (on the job). It is integral to be aware of what is most significant to the business and then align accordingly.

Maneuver – put yourself in a superior position relative to the enemy. There often are aspects of the terrain which can be leveraged to gain a maneuverability advantage in MMORPGs -- for example, if a monster has the ability to knock you back, it might be advantageous to fight with your backs against a wall. Or, if a monster has less resistance to water, then see if it can be lured to fight near a river (or your casters should utilize water-based spells). In business, maneuver is about positioning relative to competitors. In all actions, be aware of what the competition is doing and wants to do, and adjust as needed.

Unity of Command – always ensure that there is one point person who is ultimately responsible for calling the shots. It is often necessary to designate backup leaders in case the named group or raid leader becomes inaccessible or ineffective. In business situations, it is important that people understand where the buck stops.

Security – don't allow the enemy to acquire an unexpected advantage. This is about being prepared. Group and raid leaders, as much as possible, ensure that strategy and tactics are known and communicated. They put in place mitigation plans that they deem necessary. They bring the appropriate people and equipment and attack when the time is right. In business, everything is about being prepared and aware. Don't let the competitors exploit the market without having an answer. Don't rest on your laurels based on previous accomplishments. Communicate strategy to all stakeholders. Enable your people and always have an exit strategy.

Surprise – attack the enemy when and where he is least prepared. For example, if the target sleeps at night and there is an advantage to attacking him when sleeping, then factor that variable into the plan. Or, if the target walks in a certain path, and you can strike him from behind for bonus damage, then factor that in as well. Perhaps the enemy has multiple allies, and as he patrols, there are opportunities to attack him when alone. Or, perhaps the enemy casts protective spells on himself – so try to attack when they are depleted. In business, this pertains to beating the competition to the punch. Be the first to market. Deliver better than is expected.

Simplicity – the plans to achieve victory need to be as simple as possible (but not simpler). The greater the complexity of planning, the higher the likelihood that mistakes will be made. Sometimes the most simplistic strategies can be effective – to charge in and start swinging.

Morale and Exploitation are included in the nine principles of combat strategy. Exploitation is about momentum, more than just about military advantage – it is about optimizing economic, political, and other environmental factors in your favor. Morale of all guild members (or soldiers, in the military analogy, or employees, in a business analogy, etc.) speaks to their mental and emotional condition. When guild members lose morale, they can become sloppy in how they play. Healers may not strive with the same intensity and fervor to keep others alive. Warriors don't react as quickly. If the operation goes south, people want to give up. It is integral to always maintain people's fighting spirit.

It is often the leaders who are responsible for formulating and implementing strategy. They are the ones who decide what the guild/company is going to do and how they are going to do it, given their guild/company (people, culture, structure, resources, etc.) and the environment. The environment includes factors such as: competitors; the economy (market trends, suppliers, etc.); the laws and rules which govern the lands; the technologies that are available; the resources (people, items, etc.); and the external culture.

Leaders must utilize many of these factors in any strategic analysis. Some strategies which might seem innovative could be perceived or identified as exploitative to the administrators of an MMORPG, so it is important to understand the laws/rules which govern the game. For example – it is sometimes possible to maneuver into positions which prohibit a monster from being able to fight back (perhaps because it can't see the players or because the players are able to attack it through virtual walls due to bugs in code); often, however, there are rules which state that if the monster cannot legitimately fight back, then you cannot engage it. Doing so would risk a banning from the game or even deletion.

"Estimates of the number of Chinese gold farmers vary from 500,000 to over one million, as teenage drop-outs and jobless 20-somethings from poor villages or underdeveloped cities flood into the mushrooming gold-farming factories."

http://mmopub.com/2007/07/07/still-more-news-on-chinese-gold-farmers/

Communication Strategy

Online communications have changed greatly over the years. What started as the simplistic ability to chat with other users who were logged into the same computer (1970s on the Unix OS) has expanded into talking to users around the world over the internet. Voice-over-IP and video conferencing is becoming a staple of modern communications.

Part of a guild leader's communication strategy involves technology – how will the guild communicate? Instant messaging in and out of the game, threaded forums, wikis, emails, voice-over-IP, and in person "guild events" are all mechanisms by which guilds communicate. MMORPG users have always pushed the collaboration envelope. They were among the first to utilize internet-wide instant messaging software such as ICQ and AOL IM, since they needed a way to more effectively communicate and coordinate their online gaming activities.

Leaders in the real world also need to ensure proper communication strategies exist. Many of the same technologies that guilds use are great options.

Some mature guilds strive to ensure that communication lines exist internally between members and externally into the community.   Guild   leaders   occasionally   establish communication officers who are responsible for representing the guild in public forums. These often are the same people who take on the role of administering guild web sites. Communication guidelines that indicate who can talk and when, often are established prior to raids to ensure that the 80 people listening to a VoIP chat are not confused as to the directives.

It is integral to communicate frequently and repetitively. Good leaders ensure that collaboration tools are prevalent and utilized. They urge others in their guild/team to communicate. Some even make the use of collaboration technologies a prerequisite to being invited to join their guild.

The gaming environment is conducive to continually meeting new people -- either because you randomly come across them in the virtual world or because of the heavily utilized dashboards which indicate when someone is looking for a group (called PUGs, or "pick-up-groups," which are for hunting and questing partners). Some games allow teleportation options for people to move instantly from one location of the virtual world to another. This is a great mechanism to achieve instantaneous "character-to-character" (face-to-face) meetings.

The meetings that occur in MMORPGs are significantly less frequent and less formal than those in the real world. Yet, countless decisions are made, and action is taken. Collaboration technologies are so prevalent that meetings are, at the same time, both continuous and never existing - continuous in the sense that information is constantly flowing, and decisions are continually made, and never existing because gamers rarely schedule specific times and areas to share information or make decisions (which are the purposes of meetings).

I have noticed an interesting phenomenon associated with meetings and public speaking. Almost everyone becomes anxious when speaking in public. It is probably the most common phobia in the world. I would wager that some people would rather eat worms than speak in public. However, I have not noticed the phobia existing to the same degree in virtual worlds -- especially when only text communication is being used. Which begs the question, why does public speaking make people so anxious? The common reasons are that people feel that they might look foolish if they make mistakes; that they might forget what they are saying and become humiliated; that people are judging them; etc. Of course, all of those reasons would exist for virtual public speaking, as well, so I think that there is more to it. There is some aspect of seeing people, face-to-face in the real world, that is daunting and that is a significant component of the public speaking phobia. If that aspect could be conquered, perhaps the phobia would not be so prevalent.

Dashboards, as mentioned previously, are another effective mechanism for clear and effective communication. Dashboards tap into people's visual skills to quickly absorb large quantities of information. I've always thought that a "morale" dashboard would be interesting (not to take the place of face-to-face interactions). Perhaps people could quantify how they "feel" on a weekly basis (check 1, 2, etc.) The larger the group that is being led, the more something like this could come in handy.

Effective guild leaders often have communication strategies (formal or informal) and are constantly looking to increase collaboration and communication in order to improve performance. While you generally will not find written communication strategies among guild leaders in online games, you will find leaders who: understand the various communication channels at their disposal; constantly disseminate goals and objectives; ensure that people understand the communication processes and channels that are available; and ensure that communication is purposeful and timely, across all guild members.

Effective leaders in the real world should similarly strive to increase collaboration and communication in order to improve performance.

In 2005, a deadly viral in-game plague hit the World of Warcraft universe. The infection was only supposed to strike a few players on a specific high level quest, but then it began to replicate itself to other players via an in-game pet. The plague spread quickly, leaving hundreds of bodies lying in virtual streets.

http://news.bbc.co.uk/1/hi/technology/4272418.stm

Script It, Automate It

A lot of MMORPGs are filled with mundane, repeated actions. Things like: kill 20 orcs; craft 20 belts; kill 20 big orcs (did I just repeat that?). The basic formula is to do quests, kill monsters, craft items, harvest resources, and gain experience. Rinse. Repeat. "Grinding" is when you are doing the same thing over and over to grow your character (it often refers to repeatedly killing the same monsters in the same area). Most people (myself included) don't find grinding particularly enjoyable, but everyone seems to enjoy the increased power (and access to new content) that comes from growing your character.

Early in my online gaming career, I looked to automate things that were not fun or could be optimized. I started with macros – for example, instead of typing "fight orc" on the keyboard, I might just hit my F1 key, which I had mapped to automatically send "fight orc" back to the game. This was beneficial in player-vs-player, text-based online games, where speed was of the essence, and typing, rather than macro'ing, could be the difference between life and virtual death. Even today's graphical games have a text interface imbedded (often called "slash commands") beneath the beautiful 3D graphics. Using the keyboard is still the primary interface into today's MMORPGs.

After simplistic macros, I progressed to creating macros which called other macros. Then I created programs (or scripts) to play the mundane aspects of the game for me. This is now known as "botting." A Bot (short for robot) refers to a character in an online game which isn't under the control of a human player – instead, it is led by "AI," or "artificial intelligence", that has been programmed into it. It obviously is not true AI; rather, the virtual character follows simple heuristics (sets of instructions) that say, "If X happens do Y." (For example, if health gets too low, drink a potion. If there are no potions in your backpack, go buy potions. Etc.). Botting came into fashion in the late 1990s and early 2000s. In response, online game designers and companies began to institute rules that banned the use of botting or other types of programs that controlled virtual characters, because they wanted a level playing field.

A lot of repetitive actions or tasks that occur in the workplace today could be automated to greatly streamline performance. Automation should not occur merely for automation's sake – but it is important to look for ways to optimize existing processes, and automation is certainly worth considering in many situations. It never ceases to surprise me how, in the information age, there is still so much tiring grunt work that could be accomplished through automation – freeing up those individuals for more creative and productive (and fun) work. Increased automation can help in the execution of strategy.

"The government in Beijing is reported to be introducing the controls to deter people from playing (online games) for longer than three consecutive hours... 'The timing mechanism can prevent young people from becoming addicted to online games,' said Xiaowei Kou, of the General Administration of Press and Publication (GAPP), the body which regulates online gaming."

http://www.downloads.freegames.eu.com/MMORPG.html

Slay the Dragon with Half the People

Play smarter (and harder). Strategy makes all the difference between failure and success in MMORPGs, and a well-orchestrated strategy, executed by a few good players, often yields more success than a poor strategy utilizing tons of disorganized players (like "zerging," where the primary tactic is swarming the boss mob with sheer numbers of people in hopes of overwhelming it). Poor strategy can be successful, but usually at the cost of time, energy, money, and other resources (and sometimes, lives).

I rarely have subscribed to zerging tactics, unless the losses sustained would be immaterial. The harder-core the online game, the more strategy is needed, because some losses can be permanent (or at least take months to recover from) – for example, permanent equipment loss or permanent stat loss, or even permanent character death. Some of today's most popular online games have decreased the penalties associated with virtual deaths to a point where the intensity of the gaming experience has been reduced and the need for clever strategy has decreased. When recovering from death is so simplistic, many people can avoid spending much thought on strategy. Some old school online games had severe penalties, ranging from the above mentioned permanent equipment and stat loss all the way to permanent character loss (i.e., death, meaning start a new character – which is particularly nasty given the Internet connection issues). However, even though the loss from death has been decreased, the need and ability to coordinate multiple groups of people has increased.

I always have focused on how to preserve and grow our guild characters, so I always have tried to ensure that we had in place strategies that would increase our odds of success. I was very selective in my recruiting process, so I often had to devise strategies to accomplish things with fewer people. If it was normal to take 10 people to a specific battle to be successful, I would take 5. If the norm was 20, I'd try with 10. I never came across a challenge that couldn't be met with half the normally prescribed people. For me, it was fun to evaluate the situation, test multiple ways to achieve success, and then execute. I spent a lot of time testing outside-the-box strategies in games where death was impactful. The people with whom I was playing shared that same philosophy of trying to accomplish things with fewer people, though sometimes we joined with others for pure zerg-fests, when losses weren't significant.

In many guilds, most of the work is done by a minority of the people. There is almost always "dead weight" (members who are not pulling their share of the load). Sometimes it is entire guilds, led by incompetent leaders who themselves are shirking their duties. Sometimes guild members are working hard, but not on things that truly matter. They may appear significant or important, but when evaluated in terms of the goals or vision, they are completely unaligned.

The phrase "work smarter, not harder" should not be used trivially. Perhaps the right people are working smart, and hard, on appropriate activities – but they are simply understaffed due to lack of management and leadership. So, it is always beneficial to determine if the right work is being done and if it could be optimized. Are some folks doing the same repeated process daily? Can it be automated, and then could those people be repurposed elsewhere? Are they working on the most valuable activities? Is excellence the bar by which people are measured, or is mediocrity accepted? Is the competition continually being evaluated? Is strategic innovation being incentivised? I am an advocate of working smarter *and* harder.

In business, the "dragon" is a metaphor for a difficult project or situation. Most problems in the business world could effectively be navigated with half the people – assuming that they are the right people. Thus, slay the dragon with half the people.

Strategy and tactics often determine success or failure. Ten strong people working together can be more effective than thirty mediocre players playing (or working) haphazardly.

In Harbin, a city in Northeast China, gold farmers work in 12 hour shifts, earn around 1600 yuan a month. The average salary in Harbin is less than 1000 yuan per month.

http://mmopub.com/2007/07/07/still-more-news-on-chinese-gold-farmers/

Observe, Evaluate, Adopt, Improve

Understanding how the competition succeeds is important in developing new and innovative strategies. I used to spend hours of my online gaming time observing how others operated. I would evaluate what they were doing and the whys and hows of their success. If their strategies were more effective than my own, I would adopt them (or parts of them) and then improve upon them. Observe, evaluate, adopt, and improve.

The improve cycle never ceases; you continually try to identify ways to do it better, faster, and cheaper. A min/maxer by nature, I am always figuring out how to maximize the odds, minimize the risk, maximize the return, build the strongest character in the shortest time (optimize my time), etc. We definitely have amazing tools available to us. Gone are the days when information was not at one's fingertips. Now there are thousands of spoiler web-sites with deep information about online games, character-building strategies, raiding strategies, etc. If you want to beat a monster, the odds are that a YouTube video already exists that you could watch. That said, it still can be fun to push all those aids aside and simply explore new content on your own – a pristine MMORPG experience.

One can readily apply these lessons to the real world (i.e., leaders constantly should be observing, evaluating, adopting, and improving).

I subscribe to the Boy Scout Motto, "Be Prepared." For me, that means to go into any new situation with optimal protective spells and gear; to be aware of how the surroundings could be leveraged to my advantage; to have backup plans; to party (i.e., join forces) with only the best of the best; etc. Being prepared also means improving currently utilized strategies. It includes never accepting mediocrity and always striving for excellence. It means never giving up. In my 25+ years of playing online games, there was never a monster that we didn't ultimately defeat.

Summary

- Strategy is everything.

- As people and businesses mature, a greater emphasis is placed on strategy.

- In spite of the importance of strategy, important decisions frequently are made without ample consideration of strategic concerns.

- Strategies often are adaptable and always should provide tangible results.

- Strategic planning consists of having a vision of what needs to be accomplished; identifying roadblocks to achieving that vision; identifying solutions to those problems; and communication.

- Objective, offensive, mass, economy of force, maneuver, unity of command, security, surprise, and simplicity are key principles of combat strategy and business strategy.

- Leaders often are responsible for formulating and implementing strategy.

- Some strategies which might seem innovative could be perceived or identified as exploitative to the administrators of an MMORPG, so it is important to understand the laws/rules which govern the game.

- It's imperative to communicate frequently and repetitively. Good leaders ensure that collaboration tools are prevalent and utilized.

- The gaming environment is conducive to continually meeting new people.

- Meetings occur in MMORPGs significantly less frequently and less formally than in the real life workplace. Yet, countless decisions are made, and action is taken.

- Dashboards, as mentioned previously, are another effective mechanism for clear and effective communication.

- Public speaking phobias are greatly reduced in the virtual world.

- Effective leaders often have communication strategies (formal or informal) and are constantly looking to increase collaboration and communication in order to improve performance.

- More automation should be leveraged where possible and where it makes sense.

- If your business could disappear without it impacting your customers, then you had best rethink your competitive differentiation.

- More can be done (and is done) by the few. All should be focused on strategy, and excellence should be the norm.

- Observe, evaluate, adopt, and improve – is the cycle of success.

CHAPTER 7: FUTURE

How can today's leaders prepare for tomorrow? How should today's leaders operate? What are tomorrow's leaders going to be like? Read on.

Leaders Ensure Future Leadership

A successful guild can flourish for years in the online world, led by the same leader, even though a year is an eternity in the ever-changing Internet. However, most guilds last for only months, never gaining any sort of traction or sustainability. Some guild member relationships are so strong that the members will follow one another (and/or their leader) to other MMORPGs. Some of my friends and I have been playing (off and on) for decades. For me, the fun is not just about the game but, also, the people. I have developed some lasting relationships with online gamers, and I feel that we have successfully navigated some trying times together.

Almost all guilds succeed or die because of one main factor: leadership. They die because of lack of leadership, or they succeed because of the right mix of leadership and people. When guild leaders move on, guilds tend to die gradually. While some players step up to formally adopt the leadership mantle, more often than not, the guild dissolves.

I've seen guild after guild crumble because they had not planned for succession (I've been guilty of the same – although, generally, when I've left a game, I've gone with my entire guild). A guild leader might quit an MMORPG for a variety of reasons, and invariably, the guild tends to grind to a halt. The guild leaders that have longevity and sustainability as parts of their vision are the ones who proactively groom their people to ensure future leadership.

Some guild leaders even seem to fear succession planning -- they don't want to give over their "reigns of power" to anyone else. Those guilds invariably die or are successful only as long as the guild leader is in the driver's seat.

Real world leaders also need to plan for succession. They constantly need to be identifying and preparing the next-generation of leaders.

World of Warcraft was added to the World Series of Video Games, an international professional electronic sports competition in 2007.

http://en.wikipedia.org/wiki/World_Series_of_Video_Games

Balance In Everything

When I first started leading teams of people in online games, I always wanted more output: spend more time online; grow faster; etc. I didn't want their real life issues to take priority over gaming issues or over guild needs. That was a mistake.

Over time, I came to realize that people need to employ their own good judgment and play responsibly. I've seen people lose their jobs over spending too much time in games. I've known of marriages that broke up due to a spouse's inability to control time spent online. I've had friends who have spent thousands of dollars buying virtual items online. There is even a well-documented case of suicide that occurred (http://en.wikipedia.org/wiki/Shawn_Woolley) in the online gaming community. This is one of the very few isolated instances of a real-life tragedy that may have resulted from addiction to MMORPG. Future guild leaders increasingly will put emphasis on <u>balance</u> in everything – work/play/life.

I began to shift my focus from the character in the guild to the person behind the character in the guild. I now have a policy that real life always comes first, no matter what. It is important for people to know that you care more about their well being than a guild goal. And, not surprisingly, happier, more productive players lead to stronger, more sustainable guilds. Utterly obsessed players yield short term gains, but they often burn out or spiral out of control. It is the responsibility of the guild leader to ensure that guild members remain healthy.

The key is maintaining balance. Guild leaders need always to care for their people and to ensure that no one is taking the game to the extreme. No guild goal is worth destroying one's personal life – and it's the guild leader's responsibility to look after the interests of the guild members, not just the interests of the guild.

Virtual online environments are going to become commonplace in the future. Virtual shopping centers will spring up, with people controlling avatars, socializing, purchasing items (both virtually for their avatars and/or for themselves in real life). Virtual schools will be prevalent – changing from simple "online courses" to actual online environments – with virtual trees, buildings, etc, enhancing the experience. Business will take the virtual online environments by storm – providing a slew of new and innovative products and services.

As online gaming and virtual environments continue to proliferate deeper into our collective psyche (and I believe that they will), it is important for online leaders to continually bring things into perspective, encourage balance, and always care for the people behind the pixels.

It is imperative also in the real world for leaders to realize that sustainable practices must be engendered to ensure a profitable future for companies, communities, and the world. The key is balance in all.

"Everquest is renowned and berated (by some psychologists specializing in computer addiction) for its addictive qualities. Many refer to it half-jokingly as "NeverRest" and "EverCrack" (a reference to crack cocaine)."

http://en.wikipedia.org/wiki/Everquest

Ignore the Critics

The more dominant a guild becomes, the more critics will surface. There seems to be a one-to-one correlation between level of success and number of critics. Tomorrow's guild leaders will need to ignore the critics and stay true to themselves.

Communication options are abundant in the online world, and critics invariably utilize all of them to take their shots, based on: how someone runs a guild; what a guild is doing; what a guild is not doing; etc. -- the possibilities are endless. Game forums, chats, and the Internet are rife with negativity and criticism.

Countless times, I've been told that I couldn't achieve something – such as influence the direction of the game or become the dominant guild on a server. That served only as impetus for me to work harder to accomplish my goals. Critics in online games have said that I shouldn't act or be a certain way – some have said that I am too aggressive, while others have said that I'm not aggressive enough. Some have complained that developers must have given me unfair inside game information, and others have complained about what I named my guild or what raid strategies I utilized.

Critics are everywhere and often speak out of ignorance, or assumption, or just plain frustration. For some, it may even be part of their own game strategy. It is obvious and cliché, but you can't please everyone all the time – and the more influential you become in an environment, the larger the target on your back. I came to the conclusion that leaders should always remain true to themselves and their own philosophies, and everything else should be shrugged off. It is always good to listen when logical things are said, but never compromise on what you think is fair or just. Stay the path and ignore the critics.

"The U.S. intelligence community is working to develop software that will detect (terrorists) infiltrating World of Warcraft and other massive multiplayer games, according to a data-mining report from the Director of National Intelligence."

http://blog.wired.com/27bstroke6/2008/02/nations-spies-w.html

---

Have Fun

In a top-end guild, it is sometimes easy to lose sight of the fact that you are playing MMORPGs generally to have fun.

Raids can lose their luster after you have done the same thing a few dozen times to ensure that all players can get the items that they desire. It is common to hear players make comments such as, "well, gotta get back to the grind," referring to their need to do hours of mindless playing in order to get more powerful. Instead of the game being a temporary release of responsibility, it becomes just the opposite.

The future of game design needs to be cognizant of this phenomenon and compensate accordingly. The focus should be on continually making the game more fun, not more tedious. "Time sinks," such as staring at a spell book for a minute between fights to regenerate mana, should be minimized. Leverage the power of the community and create mechanisms that allow moderated content creation – let the people do the work for you, and then absorb their efforts into future releases. Rethink raid mechanics to increase the rewards for more players – get away from raid concepts where you do the same monster fifty times for fifty people. Capping character gains per day or introducing mechanisms of significantly decreased gains after an hour of play will allow "balanced" fun for those that don't utilize good judgment in their playing time. Persistent avatars (think "Sims: MMORPG") where your character continues to work/play while you are offline is probably in the future of fun gaming. A mechanism to allow for avatar offspring with traits from both "parents" should be introduced to bring a new element of fun and customization. And of course, extreme customization and the ability to become truly unique (and tangibly influence your environment) are all the futures of gaming. More 3-d interaction in the environment (i.e., a greater reliance on air strategy) also will occur. True 3-d monitors will come out someday, and thought-wave based interfaces probably will be part of the fun, next-gen gaming experience. MMORPG companies should look to partner with one another, to allow some mechanism for avatar persistence among worlds (at some degraded level of power).

Guild leaders also must acknowledge when fun is lacking in the guild. A quick way to lose players is from burn-out because the game is more of a chore than an escape into fun. Speaking purely from the retention aspect, the guild leader is responsible for injecting fun into everything as much as possible. Some guilds sponsor contests on servers (such as races between areas, game knowledge trivia quizzes, scavenger hunts, etc.); others have celebrations and traditions to create more fun. Some hold guild "team building" exercises that have everyone working together on light-hearted activities. Some guild leaders even request that the members take time away from the game to give them a breather. Also, there are guild "hall of fame" websites, which tout their guild and their members' accomplishments. Acknowledging anniversaries of the guild (or its members) is a practice that some leaders follow. Ultimately, finding humor in negative situations is something which can elevate people's moods – for example, dancing on your own corpse after the entire party has wiped will draw a few chuckles. Guild leaders realize that the future of any guild includes the basic and seemingly obvious concept of having fun.

The same can be said for the future of the business work-place. Leaders should be responsible for introducing fun into work. Fun does not mean lazy. It means increased and sustainable productivity. People simply do better when they are happy. A fun environment stimulates creativity (which often leads to innovation), reduces stress, and increases the likelihood of retaining them.

I believe that the future of many work environments will be 3D virtual work-places similar to MMORPGs. Significant companies will exist purely in virtual online worlds, and employees never will meet except as avatars. This will yield the same increased collaboration (while limiting spam) that MMORPG users see – perhaps utilizing dynamic language translation to allow users from around the world to interact more fluidly – perhaps with automatic and contextually accurate scribing; facilitating is generally easier in the online world with the ability to automatically turn down/shut off discussion hoarders. The CEO will be able easily to address everyone with his personalized avatar in whatever fun environments he wishes – rather than always flying out to meet individual business units or departments. People will login to demonstrate presence -- or perhaps calendaring systems will be tied into the environments to show where people are working. Skillset lists will be available with a simple "who" command – to identify people that could help you with particular issues. This "game-like" work environment will facilitate opportunities for sudden leadership, similar to what happens in online gaming. Constant feedback on performance should be integrated into future virtual work environments. The future is limitless.

Legendary Pictures acquired the rights to make a World of Warcraft movie with an estimated budget of over $100 million.

http://en.wikipedia.org/wiki/World_of_Warcraft

Future Leaders

Many of the guild leaders whom I have known always had an air of mystery. They didn't (seemingly) purposefully adopt a mysterious demeanor; it just seemed that they always had a bit of "je ne sais quoi" to them: what made them tick, what their backgrounds were, and what they were doing. That air of mystery (and lack of transparency) works in the online world, but not in the real world.

Everything is an opportunity for learning, and future leaders should be learning constantly. Perhaps some lessons from the virtual world can be taken and applied in the real world. Is it okay to be a boss and a buddy? Do you really need a title to be a leader? Can you be an influence change catalyst with followers? Have you defined your own statue? Are you treating people fairly but differently? Are you asking what people need? Are you leveraging the power of an emotionally impactful true story? Are you implementing traditions on your teams and injecting fun into your activities? Are you cutting out the poison when it surfaces? Are you truly trusting and being trusted?

What is the future of leadership? Leadership will continually evolve. Future leaders will leverage everything at their disposal, from technology to people, while always maintaining laser-sharp focus on strategy, which will be continually communicated. Individualized management will appreciate and acknowledge diversity. Future guild leaders will think beyond their server onto all servers, or into other games (and will strive to maintain their guilds between games and perhaps beyond games). There will be a continual trend towards moving thought away from the self and into the collective. More people will realize that they are leaders – and they will take on purposeful leadership roles.

Future leaders will be continually transforming environments and people, rather than simply maintaining in survival mode. Leaders will realize that if people are their secret sauce for competitive differentiation, they should do things for their people differently from every other company; otherwise, they will simply be on a par with everyone else.

As the boundaries between the real and the virtual become more blurred, online communities will continually become stronger social, political, and economic forces. Leaders need to be aware and prepared.

It will be imperative for future leaders to be broad generalists to be able to think beyond their standard boundaries and verticals – or they will miss opportunities for innovation and market growth. Perhaps instead of competing, they will strive to partner. The focus on cost-cutting will slowly wane as that's a losing end-game. The more self-interest prevails, the faster people will lose. If business leader focus remains on the next quarter, they are probably already on the way to losing.

Any entity (company, business, community, church, etc.) needs care and feeding to grow. Future leaders will need to become ever increasingly aware of their responsibility to "keep watch" over these entities to ensure that they continuously flourish and evolve.

Risk-taking and experimentation will increase and be rewarded – as will mechanisms to capture everyone's internal visionary spirit. Leaders will continually focus on making win/win situations for everyone's future. The leaders of tomorrow will take the realities of the current world and, working collaboratively with those around them, enable a more prosperous future for all.

Future leaders will focus even more on the people – because it's all about relationships with people. There never has been, and never will be, a single individual with all the answers – and the leaders of the future will know this and know that no one is above or below anyone else. Trust will need to increase, as will hope and faith. Future leaders will honor the past and will continually put others before themselves, starting with giving their people the best of the fruits of their efforts (the best loot).

Finally, future leaders will follow E.T.'s motto: "Be good."

Summary

- Leaders ensure future leadership.

- Almost all guilds succeed or die because of one factor: leadership.

- Ignore critics and stay true to yourself.

- Always bring fun back into the work.

- Leaders will realize that if people are their secret sauce for competitive differentiation, they will do things for their people differently from every other company.

- To ensure a future, we all need to bring sustainable practices into our daily processes.

- Balance in work and life is key to sustainability.

- Future leaders will focus more on the people.

- Future leaders will need to become ever increasingly aware of their responsibility to "keep watch" over their companies (etc.) to ensure that those companies continuously flourish and evolve.

- Future leaders, working collaboratively with those around them, will charge into the future.

APPENDIX A - MMORPGs

WHAT is an MMORPG?

An MMORPG (Massively Multiplayer Online Role Playing Game) is a computer game, played over the Internet, with (up to) thousands of simultaneous players. Most successful MMORPGs are based in a fantasy-themed universe (e.g., Lord of the Rings). MMORPGs are called "persistent worlds" because even after someone disconnects from the game, the world continues to exist. Some "Non-Player Characters," the ones under computer control, actually live virtual lives. They go to "work" in the morning (perhaps blacksmithing), sleep at night, etc. The beauty of the environment is that players can log onto the game and play as long as they like, for a few minutes or a few hours at a time. The requirements to play an MMORPG are minimal: a computer, an internet connection, a recurring fee (approximately $15/month), and the game client itself (a one-time fee ranging from $20 to $60).

"Role playing" (in MMORPGs) refers to adopting the role of a character in a fantastical setting. These settings (or worlds) are created by teams of software professionals, including writers, designers, programmers, and musicians. A person's character is visually represented (on the monitor) based on his race (such as elf, dwarf, etc.) and what he is wearing or using (platemail, a shield, etc.) A person selects a class for his character or avatar (such as wizard, thief, or warrior) and often can choose from multiple professions (such as blacksmith, farmer, alchemist, or miner) to further customize him. Some MMORPGs don't utilize classes and, instead, opt for a more open-ended "skill-based" system, which can allow for greater customization but also leads to more difficulty in game balancing.

Characters navigate throughout the history-laden virtual worlds via a variety of ways, which include walking and running, riding mounts (such as horses, gryphons, dragons, etc.), flying, via boats (from small sail-boats to massive warships), and even teleporting. The experience is purposefully meant to be immersive.

Most players in MMORPGs focus on adventuring, which includes exploring new locations, killing monsters or other characters, and completing elaborate quests. Adventuring yields "experience points," which players accumulate to grow stronger. At various "experience levels," a character can learn new and more powerful abilities, which, in turn, give him the opportunity to adventure in more dangerous areas, and the cycle never ends except when companies stop adding new content for people to enjoy. Character growth and development is key to what makes MMORPGs intriguing (e.g., being able to adopt virtual personas and play them to become more powerful).

The social aspect of online gaming is another significant focus of MMORPGs. There is constant interaction with other people from around the world, often working collaboratively together. Sometimes people choose not to adventure, preferring a leisurely chat with their friends, as on a casual telephone call.

MMORPGs feature complex economies, where equipment, currency, characters, real estate, and resources are bartered and sold within the game. Also, some virtual items recently have been sold for real money outside of the games, creating new business opportunities for enterprising individuals and companies – acquiring and then selling virtual items for actual money. Some people even make their living by working as merchants in virtual economies – "Chinese gold farmers," who often are employed in game "sweatshop"-like conditions, play for 12 hours a day in order to sell virtual gold to western players through websites.

WHERE did MMORPGs come from?

MMORPGs often are seen as the natural evolution of pen-and-paper dice games, such as "Dungeons and Dragons." Shortly after D&D came out, text-based online adventure games became popular in the form of dial-up modem Bulletin Board System games (BBSs) and Multi-User Dungeons (MUDs).

It wasn't until the late 1990s, with games such as Ultima Online and Everquest, that technology matured to the point where beautiful 3-dimensional graphics and sound could be incorporated into online text gaming to make environments incredibly more immersive.

The general timeline for some interesting aspects of gaming (and computers) is as follows:

1960s Spacewar. Developed on PLATO at MIT. Up to 2 people on a networked computer played simultaneously. This game basically was a 2-dimensional game which involved spaceships trying to shoot one another.

1973 Airfight. Developed on PLATO. Airfight was 3-dimensional and potentially inspired what later became Microsoft's Flight Simulator.

1976 Apple is founded by Steve Jobs, Steve Wozniak, and Ronald Wayne.

1978 MUD1/Advent/Dungen. Roy Trubshaw and Richard Bartle create the first MUD (Multi-User Dungeon) on a PDP-10. MUD1 was a simple text-based adventure game where people could move between areas (called rooms) and chat with other people via simple commands.

1978 CBBS (Bulletin Board System) goes online developed by Ward Christenson. CBBS was a system that allowed a virtual community to come together and post messages to one another. Connection was achieved over modems (110 and 300 BAUD modems at that time).

1980 Dungeons of Kesmai is created by Kelton Flinn and John Taylor. Dungeons of Kesmai used ASCII graphics to represent a 2-dimensional fantasy realm. It supported up to 6 simultaneous users on a Z-80.

1980s BBS (and "door") games are developed and played via dial-up modems. These start with people playing in the same world at different times and then evolve to multiple people playing simultaneously.

1982   Scott E. Fahlman first uses the :-) emoticon in an email on a Carnegie Mellon University BBS.

1982   Commodore 64 is released.

1984   Trade Wars is created – first written in BASIC for the TRS-80; then ported to the PC as a popular BBS door game played by modem.

1984   Islands of Kesmai is released on Compuserve. IoK was a fantasy-based, 2-dimensional, graphical ORPG. It launches at $12/hour to play.

1987   Gemstone RPG is released on Genie (as Gemstone][). This was a popular text-based pay-for-play MUD.

1990   DIKU MUDs are created by Sebastian Hammer, Tom Madsen, Katja Nyboe, Michael Seifert, and Hans Henrik at Datalogisk Institut Københavns Universitet (DIKU), the Department of Computer Science at the University of Copenhagen. This was one of the earliest and most popular MUD code-bases released, and it was extremely influential (at least from my perspective) on future MMORPGs, including Everquest, World of Warcraft, and Ultima Online.

1991   The Shadow of Yserbius is published by Sierra Online. SoY was a popular graphical fantasy theme-based MUD, pay-to-play. It supported up to 60 people simultaneously.

1992   Kingdom of Drakkar. Pay-to-play over the internet. Supported hundreds of players simultaneously. Player base of a few thousand players.

1996   Meridian 59. This MMORPG had 3-dimensional, first-person view graphics, allowed up to 250 people per server to play simultaneously, and spread out over 12 servers. Approximately 12,000 subscribers.

1997   Ultima Online is released by gaming veteran Richard Garriott (a.k.a., "Lord British"). This was a top-down, "3/4" view MMORPG with approximately 200,000 subscribers.

1998   Lineage: Top-down, 2-dimensional game. 3.5 million subscribers. It recorded over 300,000 simultaneous connections.

1999   Everquest.   Beautiful   3-dimensional   graphics. Approximately 450,000+ subscribers.

2001   Dark Age of Camelot, Anarchy Online, and Ultima Online 2 are released.

2002   Final Fantasy XI is released – first game to allow console and PC players to play together.

2003   Lineage // is released.

2004   World of Warcraft is released. Approximately 10 million subscribers. Currently the most popular pay-for-play game in the world.

2007 Tabula Rasa is released – a new Sci-Fi MMORPG developed by Richard Garriott.

WHEN do people play MMORPGs?

Since MMORPGs feature persistent universes, most people can play whenever they have free time, such as after work or school. From beginning to end, some challenges in MMORPGs can demand multiple hours to complete, so people plan their schedules accordingly. I personally try to restrict myself to playing when my family is asleep (late at night or early in the morning), though I'm sometimes guilty of breaking my own guidelines. The overall number of hours which I dedicate to entertainment remains fairly static – so, if I am deeply entrenched in online gaming, I simply watch less television or spend less time with other hobbies.

WHY do people play MMORPGs?

There are a variety of factors that motivate people to play MMORPGs. The primary ones tend to revolve around achieving something (character growth, solving puzzles, completing quests, etc.), socializing (interacting with players around the world), and/or role-playing (which is the root of online gaming – absorbing yourself in a character in a brave new virtual world). It's simply fun.

Today's MMORPGs go far beyond just destroying monsters. Now characters can focus on crafting, harvesting, diplomacy, and a variety of other activities. Some choose to live their virtual lives without ever engaging in combat (though they are still a minority). Many people play the virtual market, buying and selling in online marketplaces. Ultimately, there are many reasons for becoming part of the MMORPG phenomenon – basically, they involve whatever a person finds entertaining.

Speaking about motivation from a Maslowian perspective, MMORPGs can satisfy love and belonging needs (via friendships), esteem needs (achievement, the respect of others), and self-actualization needs (morality, creativity, problem-solving, etc.) There also are needs that relate directly to the avatar (rather than to the person playing the avatar). A player can derive vicarious satisfaction from seeing to the needs of his avatar; e.g., basic physiological needs (food, water, even air to breathe) and safety/security needs (which are about surviving and progressing in an online gaming environment).

The general public has had multiple reactions towards MMORPGs, running the gamut from huge praise to absolute disdain. Some see MMORPGs as great ways to socialize, while others see them as addictive time-sinks that kill productivity in real life – I would argue that they are at least more productive and social than watching television. The truth is probably somewhere in between. Recent attempts to classify MMORPGs as addictive have failed. The future of gaming should probably include forced (not optional) constraints to limit play-time – for example, allowing only one hour of "growth" per day on a character (probably combined with mechanisms for offline growth). Then again, perhaps that would be an infringement on individual rights.

HOW do people play MMORPGs?

Online gaming companies have made it very simple for new players to get into the game. After the game is installed, and after a simple registration process (which often includes using a credit card for recurring payments), the game is launched. The standard steps for playing include: naming a character (something that isn't offensive or derogatory), picking a race (elf, dwarf, etc.), a class (wizard, warrior, etc.), and then picking a server (some online games are split into multiple servers based on geographic location – so Europe has servers, North America has its own, etc. – many games will make server recommendations based on which ones give the least latency).

The experience truly begins as one logs into a server and is immediately presented with a lush virtual environment, accompanied by an incredible musical score. Player- and computer-controlled characters often are seen moving about, interacting with the environment. The keyboard and mouse are the current mechanisms for interfacing with the game. It's that simple.

Most games have tutorials which walk people through basic activities such as movement, combat, chatting, questing, and a variety of other hand-holding exercises to quickly make the experience immersive. After the basic aspects of gaming have been mastered, characters tend to leave the comparatively safe confines of the starting "newbie" areas (or zones) and begin to explore the rest of the world.

WHO plays MMORPGs?

As I previously mentioned, there seem to be no social, political, or economic bounds in terms of who is playing online games. I have played with skateboarders, yuppies, doctors, retirees, lawyers, drug dealers, pit bull fighters, married people, football players, mothers, executives, janitors, surgeons, graduate students, etc. The only constraint seems to be a computer and broadband access (and interest and, perhaps, time). In my own experience, there are definitely more males than females playing online games, although the percentages are getting closer as time progresses.

According to Nick Yee, a Stanford Ph.D who studies online games and virtual environments, the average age of the MMORPG player is 26; 50% of MMORPG players work full-time; 36% of players are married; and the average MMORPG player games 22 hours per week. I would wager that hard-core raiders play approximately 40 hours per week. That might sound excessive (and it is), but to put into context how people spend their leisure time, the average American watches approximately 28 hours per week of television. Some famous people are known to play MMORPGs, including Boston Red Sox pitcher Curt Schilling and Philadelphia Phillies center fielder Doug Glanville, both of whom are Everquest players. Comedian Dave Chappelle, actor Robin Williams, and basketball star Yao Ming are all avid World of Warcraft players. Bottom line, many types of people play MMORPGs.

APPENDIX B - /whoami

I began playing computer games on my uncle's Apple // computer in about 1978. He was an undergrad at the University of Oregon and I was 7 years old. I was fascinated by his computer and his acoustic coupler modem – I loved watching it connect to the various computer systems out in the world.

Over the next few years, I cajoled my way into getting an Apple II+, a Commodore 64, and an Apple //c. My first modem was an acoustic coupler CAT modem, and then I upgraded to a Hayes Smartmodem 300 baud (then a 1200, 2400, etc.) My online gaming experience started with BBS games. BBSs (Bulletin Board Systems) are applications that allow people to dial in and connect, over phone lines, to perform a variety of functions, including reading news, chatting, and playing games (with other users). Initially, BBSs allowed only one person at a time to connect to them –

however, they quickly progressed to allow multiple simultaneous connections.

I played online games such as Trade Wars and Proving Grounds and also started MUDding. Many games were turn-based, allowing three calls per day – resetting at midnight. I set up my demon-dialer so that I could be the first person to call past midnight – so my character could become stronger sooner than everyone else's.

From online games, I learned to think and act "outside–the-box," i.e., to do things in ways that were different from what everyone else was doing. An example is the way in which I was playing Proving Grounds. Proving Grounds featured fantasy-based user-against-user battles, a gambling casino, jousting, and much more. It had a character advancement system that allowed an allocation of attributes among strength, intelligence, and agility (if memory serves). It had a "Top 100" adventurers list, which listed people's attributes, win/loss ratios, etc. I noticed a pattern among the strongest players – they all had similar stats – high strength for damage, medium points in agility for jousting, and low intelligence – which is where hit points (or health, i.e. the amount of damage you can sustain before death) came from.

You were allowed 3 calls per day to that particular Proving Grounds BBS, and you could joust 3 times per call – and after you had won a few jousts, you gained attributes that you could add to your abilities – and when you reached a certain threshold of experience, then you could "level up" (move up to the next level) to gain even more attributes. But, leveling up was a choice, nothing that was forced.

Most people would level up as soon as they could, because attributes were gained automatically that way. I devised a strategy to purposefully stay at level one and simply keep putting the attributes that I gained from jousting into my intelligence. It also kept me off the leaderboard, which meant that no one was gunning for me to take me down. My strategy was to get to 700 intelligence at level 1, and then level up, having exponentially more hit points (health) than any of the competitors. The strategy worked, and a couple months after I started playing the game, I suddenly went from not being on the top 100 to rocketing to the #1 spot in just a few days. People thought I had cheated – but I had simply utilized the system in a manner different from anyone else. I was 12 or 13 at the time.

Game after game, I enjoyed strategizing and trying different approaches to achieve success. It was something I learned early on, and I still follow that philosophy today.

I also came to realize that seemingly everyone was playing for himself in BBS games. I began to communicate with other online gamers in order to orchestrate our actions so that we could dethrone more powerful, longer-time players. I quickly realized how powerful it was to mobilize a group of people towards achieving a singular goal relative to doing it alone. We collaboratively would take games by storm and dominate the people who played alone.

My gaming continued through high school and college. Xtrek (a 2-dimensional, networked Star Trek game) was big, and text-based MUDs were everywhere. I graduated from Carnegie Mellon University with a B.S. in Mathematics and Computer Science in 1993. Graphical MUDs were just coming into existence, and I played all the free ones.

The first real pay-for-play online game I tried was "Kingdom of Drakkar." I started playing that in 1993, when I landed my first job out of college as a C++ programmer for Dynamix, a subsidiary of Sierra. Dynamix was known for games such as Red Baron, Front Page Sports, Tribes, and a few others -- Sierra was best known for its King's Quest series. I worked on Dynamix's first networked game, Battledrome. I played Drakkar quite a bit, even though it cost anywhere from $4/hour (if you connected by the Internet, which was just gaining the world's attention) to $8/hour (if you connected directly by modem).

The time commitment needed to grow powerful in Drakkar was significant, and I was putting in long hours at work, so I eventually wrote a program to play Drakkar for me. The script that I created moved my character in the game, killed monsters, looted the treasure from them, trained, and performed a variety of other actions. I integrated my script with an artificial intelligence therapist program (like "Eliza"). It was fun watching other people interact with my avatar. This is what the conversations were like with my character (named Cricket):

"Hey Cricket, how are you doing?", they would write.

"Does that question interest you?" my script would respond.

"Huh? Sure, why else would I ask? Are you smoking dope?"

"Would you prefer if I were not smoking dope?" it would send back.

The conversations would go on like that for a while, and it always cracked me up. I also began to sell the virtual goods that my character gained from scripting for real life currency. The money I made from selling in-game items covered the cost to play the game and still left me with a tidy little profit. Even more exciting was the fact that my character was getting so strong (playing 24 hours a day) that he began to be able to accomplish things that entire guilds of other players could not. I began to sell items in the game for hundreds of dollars. It was a blast playing with my guild ("Fate").

I eventually sold that character for $5,000 in 1994/95, when I grew tired of monitoring the script (I had programmed in different sounds to play based on what was happening in the game, so I could leave it running at night). I sold the script itself to a variety of people for a few hundred dollars per person. Before I sold the character, I had a garage sale of his items (some of which were artifacts) and netted another $3,000 from doing that. In total, I amassed approximately $12,000 - $15,000 in today's dollars (2007/2008). Pretty good, considering that I was selling 0s and 1s in a database. As a frame of reference, this was years before the existence of Ultima Online, Everquest or World of Warcraft.

It should be noted, also, that this was years before gaming companies began banning scripting programs. Many MMORPGs now state, in their end-user license agreements, that scripting is not allowed. I came back to Drakkar a couple years later when I heard that they had changed from pay-per-hour to pay-per-month. I actually had a character deleted in that game for gaining skill while grouped with scripters. So, I started a new character, formed a new guild, and eventually, we became the dominant guild – a title which we held for many years until we all decided to leave the game.

While I was playing "Drakkar," I was also heavily into MUDs. "Sojourn" was one of my favorites (DIKU variant) – and I enjoyed many hours with my group of friends there. Another favorite was a PVP (Player versus Player) MUD called Mortal Conquest (as well as many of its offshoots), and the guild that I formed dominated the competition.

I decided to make a change in my work life. My friends thought that I was crazy leaving the gaming industry -- it was a mini-Hollywood, after all, working with musicians, artists, directors, actors, actresses, etc. But, it was time for me to move on. My brother-in-law at the time suggested that I go into IT consulting because "you know computers and you actually have a personality." I think that he was complimenting me. This was around the time that some of the next-gen MMORPGs came out, including Myrdian 59, Ultima Online, and Everquest.

I joined a systems integrator consulting company, called Emerald Solutions, started with consulting, and then branched into technical architecture. I also co-founded an investment club, Helvetica LLC. All the while, I continued playing online games, and one of my favorites was Everquest.

Everquest was something special. It reminded me of a DIKU MUD, but with amazing 3-dimensional graphics. I joined a guild, called "Fires of Heaven," and we dominated our server (and, to be honest, all servers at that time). I got bored after I had hit the character level cap and we had conquered all the content the game had to offer, so I moved on to other games.

I left Emerald Solutions to form a new dot-com company (Help-1) with two other individuals, as a spin-off of Ziba Design (the guys who designed the Microsoft natural "split" keyboard, among other things). We wrote the business plan, met with angels/VC, etc. Our timing wasn't hot (the market was tanking with the dot-com fizzle), but it was a great learning experience. I kept playing online games.

At about that time, I was recruited, as a Technical Architect, to join a new start-up, called Vector SCM (a subsidiary of CNF, which was later rebranded as Con-way). I later became Manager of the Architecture team and then became a member of a larger Enterprise Architecture team. I continued with MUDs and other online games, such as Never Winter Nights (NWN), where I joined a guild, called "ZAR," and played with some of my old college friends.

A "next gen" MMORPG, called Vanguard, was released, so I tried it out. I formed a guild, called "Primal" and then merged with another guild, called "Pain" (I became an officer in "Pain" and we dominated the competition – and to this day, we still own most of the spots on guild leader boards). But, after dominating the top spots, I moved on.

Currently, I am a Senior Manager leading a team of Enterprise Architects for Con-way (a $4.7 billion freight transportation and logistics services company, voted #1 on the 2007 InformationWeek 500, and named FORTUNE magazine's "Most Admired Company" in Transportation and Logistics for 2007; also, voted as one of Silicon Valley's five "Most Admired Companies" in 2008 based on research done by Renaissance Publications and Digest Television, which included feedback from employees, customers, and business partners). We are the strategy guys (and gals) in IT (Information Technology, also known as Business Technology, BT).

I am 37 as I write this and it's hard to believe that I've been gaming for approximately 30 years and serving and leading people in online games for about 25. I remember having a conversation with my current manager, wherein I jokingly mentioned that I should write a book based on the leadership lessons that I had learned from online gaming. He had no idea what I was talking about, so I divulged a bit of my history. He thought that it was fascinating and said that I should do it.

So there you have it. Most of what I write about is my own anecdotal experience -- my personal history playing online games. There are countless other histories of player experiences that would surely paint different perspectives. This represents my own thoughts based on what I have witnessed.

Again, the primary purpose of this book is to share leadership lessons that I have learned from playing online games and to show how these lessons might apply to the real world. I hope that through my description and discussion of online gaming, I have contributed some useful insights into the art of leadership.

-jeon

jeon.rezvani@gmail.com

APPENDIX C – MMORPG Dictionary

<3: Love or heart.

1337: Elite.

1H: One-handed weapon. For example, a dagger.

2H: Two-handed weapon. For example, a spear.

AC: Armor Class. This is for defense – the amount of armor a character is wearing. Armor generally reduces the amount of damage taken or makes a character more difficult to injure.

AC/AC2: Asheron's Call (2), an MMORPG.

Add: When another monster joins an already existing battle.

Addon: Custom graphical user-interface written by a player.

AE: Area Effect (also known as AOE, Area of Effect). An action which affects an area, rather than a single target.

AFAIK: As Far As I Know.

AFK: Away From Keyboard (i.e., I'm busy for a moment).

AFKFAS: Away From Keyboard For A Second.

Aggro: Aggression or Aggressive. This either refers to an actual monster that is hostile towards you, or it refers to the amount of aggression a monster has built up towards you – and the higher the aggression, the higher the likelihood that he will attack you.

Aggro radius/range: How close you can get to a monster before it attacks.

AGI: Agility.

AI: Artificial Intelligence. See NPC.

AKA: Also Known As.

Alt: Alternate (see Avatar). An alternate character (usually lower level) on your account other than your main character.

AO: Anarchy Online, an MMORPG.

AOE: Area of Effect. See AE.

AP: Attack Power. Can mean a variety of things, e.g., how much damage a character can inflict, or the probability of hitting a monster, or some permutation therein.

AR: Attack Rating. See AP.

ATM: At The Moment (i.e., for now).

Attribute: A statistic representing a character's mental or physical ability, such as strength, intelligence, etc.

Avatar: The character that you are playing (often a graphical representation).

B/F: Boyfriend.

BAF: Bring A Friend. This generally means that more help is needed.

Bait: The person in the party who will attempt to lure the monster.

BBIAB: Be Back In A Bit.

BBL: Be Back Later.

Bind: A "safe" location, also known as a character's home. This is the place to which a character can teleport, or it's the location where he is resurrected if he dies.

Bind Spot: See Bind.

Bio: Biological. Used when players say "bio break, brb," or "I need to use the restroom, I'll be right back."

BOE: Bind On Equip. This refers to items which are then owned (and can be used only) by the first person who wears or uses them.

BOP: Bind on Pickup. This refers to items which are then owned (and can be used only) by the first person who touches them.

Boss (Mob): A very powerful monster, sometimes at the end of a quest.

Bot: A robot, or script, which plays a character in the place of a human being. Often a 3rd-party program.

Box/Boxing: Playing multiple computers (and characters) at the same time by the same person. For example, "I'm 2-boxing" means that I'm playing two characters on two computers at the same time.

BRB: Be Right Back.

Broken: Not working, often a quest.

BRT: Be Right There.

BTW: By The Way.

Buff: .A temporary protective spell cast on a character, often increasing his attributes or resistances.

Build: The make-up of a character – often used when describing how a player specialized and customized his character's abilities.

Camping: Waiting in an area, usually killing a specific monster/player over and over.

Carebear: Players that help other players to kill monsters (instead of other players) in environments which are created to kill other players.

Caster: Short for spell-caster or someone who does significant spell damage from a distance.

CC: Crowd Control. Controlling something to render it useless; for example, CC'ing a monster so that it cannot attack the party; or CC'ing something by making it fall asleep.

Character: See Avatar.

Charm: A common CC (Crowd Control) mechanism.

Cheese: Cheating or doing something that is either shady or in poor taste.

Clan: Another name for guild.

Class: Character type; usually fits into a role (such as healer, damage do-er, etc.).

Con: Constitution; or a monster's danger relative to your character's level; presented as a color rating; i.e., gray = cakewalk; green = should be easy for you to win; yellow = it will be a challenge for you to win; red = you have almost no chance to win.

CR: Corpse Run. In many games, after you die, you need to run back to your corpse to either get your equipment or to restore some lost experience you suffered due to the death.

Crafting: A profession, in MMORPGs, that involves creating new items from resources (for example, a jeweler or blacksmith).

Crit: Critical. Refers to scoring a "critical" hit, which does significant damage. It also can refer to your character.

Critter: A weak monster (or simply another name for monster).

CYA: See You Around.

Cyber: Having adult conversations online.

DAoC: Dark Age of Camelot, an MMORPG.

DC: Disconnected (also DC'ed). Usually refers to a character who has become inactive yet potentially still remains in the game until the server disconnects him.

DD: Direct Damage. A spell that does damage immediately (rather than over time, such as poison).

Debuff: The opposite of Buff. A temporary spell cast on a character, often decreasing his attributes or resistances.

Ding: Used when a player has increased his experience to the next level. This originated in Everquest, in which a "ding" sound was played when a character reached the next experience level.

DKP: Dragon Kill Points. A system used by some guilds to reward treasure to their guild members.

DOT: Damage-Over-Time. A spell that does damage over a period of time – such as a disease or poison spell.

DPS: Damage–Per-Second. Often refers to classes whose role in a party is doing damage (i.e., a "DPS Class"), or it refers to a way to describe the rate at which something or someone does damage; for example, a 20 DPS weapon has the potential of doing 80 points of damage in 4 seconds (with all other variables set aside).

Drop: Often refers to the treasure that monsters possess. Could refer, also, to a character who has disconnected.

Druid: A hybrid class, often part healer and part DPSer.

Dupe: Duplicate. This refers to an exploit in MMORPGs wherein a player duplicates (either purposefully or inadvertently) something; "I duped my sword" would mean that a player somehow (because of a bug in the program code) managed to get two of the same sword when he previously had only one.

Emote: An action which lets a player act out his feeling or mood – such as laughing, crying, being angry, etc. The avatar of the character often has an accompanying animation.

End-Game: The parts of an MMORPG designed for the most powerful characters.

Epic: Usually refers to something that is very difficult; or it refers to a very powerful item.

EQ: Everquest, an MMORPG.

Evac: Evacuate. Often a spell used to teleport all party members out of a dangerous situation.

Exp (XP): Experience. Points collected by a character, often for killing monsters, finishing quests, and exploring new areas. After certain experience point levels are reached, a character increases his level.

Exploit (Sploit): Doing something in a manner that wasn't intended by the game designers (such as duping), because it significantly hurts the balance of the game.

Faction: A numeric score on your character which refers to your "standing" with a particular group of monsters or people – e.g., do they view you favorably or with disdain.

Fanboi: A person who is such a fan of the game that he will never acknowledge any issues or problems with it. Usually a derogatory term.

Farm: To repetitively do the same activity (such as farming for improved faction; or farming a particular monster for his treasure).

Fear Kite: A strategy using a fear spell to expel a monster from you, while at the same time, doing damage to it.

FFA: Free For All. A treasure distribution mechanism which allows anyone to take an item from a monster once it has been killed.

Flaming (Flame War): In essence, posting an insult against someone else (e.g., calling them an idiot).

FM: Full Mana. Used to signify when a spell caster has regenerated all of his spell energy.

Fodder: Easy to kill monsters.

FPS: Frames-Per-Second. The number of frames your computer (or graphics card) can render each second. The higher the frame-rate or frames-per-second, the smoother the animation looks.

FTL: For The Loss. Something that will ultimately cause loss or failure (for example, "ga and use Ice spells on the Ice Worm FTL").

FTW: For The Win (see FTL).

GA: Go Ahead.

Gank: Gang Kill. Used when a group of players works together to kill a more powerful character; or when a higher level character kills a significantly lower level character. It also can be used to mean a surprise attack.

GG: Good Game.

Gimped: Something that is (or has been made) underpowered.

GJ: Good Job.

GL: Good Luck (can also be an acronym for Guild Leader).

GM: Guild Master. See Guild Leader. Can also mean Game Master, the MMORPG employees who monitor the game and answer certain player questions.

Gratz (Grats): Congratulations.

Green: See Con.

Grey (Gray): See Con.

Griefer: Someone who causes grief to other players, often by player-killing much weaker players.

Grinding: See Farm(ing).

GTG: Good To Go.

Guild: An organized team of people that work together (often having the same principles, goals, and values).

Guild Leader (GL): The leader of a guild.

Guildie: A member of a guild.

Healer: A class which exists primarily to keep others alive.

Health: A stat that often refers to the amount of damage a character can sustain before he is killed.

Hit Points (HP): See Health.

HOT: Heal-Over-Time. An ability to continually heal over a period of time.

HTS: Hard To Sell.

IIRC: If I Recall Correctly.

IMHO: In My Humble Opinon.

Inc: Incoming. E.g., "Add inc!" (another monster is joining the battle and will attack us!).

Instance: An instantiation (or unique area) of a particular dungeon for a group of players. Non-instanced areas means that everyone plays in the same area at the same time rather than in a unique area created just for them.

Imm: Immortal. Also known as someone who helps manage or administer the game and who has powers and abilities beyond those that player characters can achieve.

Int: Intelligence (a commonly used stat/attribute).

I Win Button: Using something (or an ability) that is overpowered is jokingly referred to as using your "I Win Button."

JK (J/K): Just Kidding.

Kite: Killing in Transit. A strategy where a monster chases you (but cannot hit you) while you inflict damage upon it. See Fear Kite for a reverse kite (i.e., instead of it chasing you, it is running away scared).

KK: Ok Cool.

KOS: Killed On Sight. When something is attacked at the instant it is seen.

KS: Kill Stealing. To kill a monster that someone else started to kill, thus stealing the credit for the kill (often seen as underhanded).

Lag: A slow internet connection that leads to a slow (choppy) game.

Lair: The home of a powerful monster.

LD: Link Dead. When a player is disconnected from the game (sometimes inadvertently; for example, when an Internet connection drops).

Leech: Someone who joins a group and benefits without contributing anything in return (perhaps he joins a much stronger party, or perhaps he is simply doing nothing productive).

Leeroy Jenkins: A player who rushes into a bunch of monsters and aggros them before the rest of the party members are ready (usually resulting in the death of everyone).

Leet: Elite. See 1337.

Level: The power of a character, usually in numeric format (such as, "I'm level 25 (of 50)."

LFG: Looking For Group. This is commonly used in public chat channels in the game to signify that a player wishes to find a group to join (to accomplish harder tasks, kill more difficult monsters, etc).

LFM: Looking For More. A group leader often calls this out in public chat channels when they need more party members to accomplish their goals.

LMAO: Laughing My Ass Off.

Log: To exit the game. Could also refer to "game logs," which are audit files that record various things that have transpired in the game.

LOL: Laughing Out Loud.

LOM: Low On Mana. A healer might say "LOM" to tell the rest of the party that he won't be able to heal for much longer.

Loot (Lewt): Treasure.

Loot Ho (Loot Whore): Someone who always wants all the treasure.

LOS: Line Of Sight. When a target is visible and not obstructed by any obstacles.

Lowbie: A low level character.

MA: Main Assist. The person that everyone else in the raid (or party) will assist (i.e., they will attack the same thing that he is attacking).

Macro: Creating a key combination (such as CTRL-M) that issues multiple commands at once.

Main: The main character that someone plays. (See Alt).

Mana: Magical Energy (used up as you cast spells, and replenished over time or by drinking potions).

Mats: Short for materials (usually for crafting items).

Meat Shield. Often the warrior, whose purpose is to draw the attention of all the monsters away from characters with less health and less defense. Also known as a Tank.

Med(ding): Meditating. In some games, it's a state into which a character enters; used to regain mana.

Melee: Close range combat.

Mez/Mes: Mesmerize (see CC).

Min/Max (ing/er): When someone optimizes what they do in order to become as powerful as possible.

Mitigation: Often said as "Damage Mitigation," or an amount of damage that a particular type of armor absorbs (so platemail would have more mitigation than leather armor).

ML: Master Looter. The person who distributes all the treasure.

MMORPG: Massively Multiplayer Online Role Playing Game.

MOB: Mobile Object. Is simply a Monster (a term taken from MUDDing).

Mod: A moderator (such as a GM), or an Addon.

MT: Main Tank. The raid (or party) member whose responsibility it is to keep the most dangerous monster(s) focused on himself. Can refer also to "Meant Tell," which is used when someone speaks to the wrong person accidentally.

MUD: Multi-User Dungeon. The pre-cursor (often text based) online multiplayer game to MMORPGs.

Mule: A character (or account) created for the sole purpose of holding extra items and treasure. Also called a "banker."

Multi: See Box(ing).

Named: A particular monster that has an actual name that is often stronger than the monsters that surround him. For example, if there are a bunch of "Orcs," and one is named "Orc King Gru'lash," then he would be the named.

Need Before Greed: A looting system which prioritizes people who need an item higher than those who simply want the item.

Nerf(ed): See Gimp(ed).

Ninja(loot): When someone takes treasure from a killed monster either very quickly or when they shouldn't have (i.e., they stole it from someone else).

Noob/N00b/Newb/Newbie: An inexperienced person (or someone new to MMORPGs).

NP: No problem.

NPC: Non-Player Character. A game character that is being controlled by the server, not by a player.

Nuke: To unload a significant amount of damage on something ("Nuke the named!")

OMG: Oh My God.

OMW: On My Way.

On Me: A statement that is made when a monster is attacking a particular person.

OOC: Out Of Character. A chat channel often used for discussion about non-game related things.

OOM: Out Of Mana (See LOM).

OOR: Out Of Range.

OT: Off Tank. This designation is used by someone who is trying to keep the attention of a monster (or monsters) other than the MT's monster.

OWNZ: Owns. To defeat something (or when something is stronger than something else). Also known as "PWNZ," probably due to the fact that P and O are next to each other on QWERTY keyboards.

Pally: Paladin (a tank/healer hybrid class).

Party: A group of players journeying and fighting together.

Patch: The process that occurs when the game's computer files are upgraded. Patch notes are the documentation that details some of the changes.

PB: Point Blank.

PC: Player Character (as opposed to NPC). A character controlled by a player.

Pet: An NPC that is being controlled by another NPC or by a Player (for example – a Demon might have a Succubus as a pet or minion)

Phat Lewtz: A slang term used to describe good treasure.

PK: Player Kill. When one player kills another player.

PM: Private Message.

Pop: Repopulate. When a monster respawns.

Pot: Potion.

Power-leveling: Leveling a character faster than is normally possible (for example, using a higher level character to help you; also used to describe a new business model whereby you outsource the playing of your character to someone else – a growing business in China).

Proc: Procedure. When an item activates a spell ability (for example, an "Ice Sword" might have a chance to "proc" an icestorm spell).

PST: Please Send Tell.   Used when a player is asking others to communicate with him regarding something (for example, someone playing a healer class might say "PST if you need a healer!")

PUG: Pick-Up-Group. A group of players that have joined together on an ad-hoc basis, usually to complete a quest or kill a monster.

Pull: To aggro monsters in a controlled fashion.

PVE: Player Versus Environment. MMORPGs where there is no player-vs-player combat (it's all player-vs-monsters).

PVP: Player Versus Player (see PVE).

PWNZ: See Ownz.

QFT: Quoted For Truth.

QQ: An emoticon used to signify crying.

R: Ready (also RDY).

Race: Dwarf, Elf, Gnome, etc.

Raid: Several groups of players working together to overcome any number of challenging obstacles, which invariably includes fighting an end-game monster.

Raid Boss: A challenging monster, often the most difficult in the area (Boss Mob).

Raid Leader/Hunt Master: The person directing all the groups in battle, usually against a Boss Mob.

Rebuff: To recast "buffs" that have expired.

Red: See Con.

Regen: Regenerate. Usually it refers to the recovery of lost health (hit points), mana, etc. It also can mean Pop.

Reroll: To create a new character.

Respawn: See Pop.

Rez (Res): To resurrect (bring someone back to life).

RL: Real Life (or IRL, In Real Life).

ROFL: Rolling On the Floor Laughing.

ROFLMAO: Rolling On the Floor Laughing My Ass Off.

Roll: A term used to signify a random roll of virtual dice (the winner getting the treasure).

Rollback: This is when a patch is removed in order to take the game to a previous state (or when a character is set back to a previous point in time because of a bug or because of cheating).

Root: To trap something in place, so that it cannot move. A form of CC.

RP: Role-play.

Skele: Skeleton.

SMAT: Send Me A Tell.

Slave: See Pet.

Solo: The act of playing alone; or, accomplishing something without outside help.

Soulbound: An item that cannot be traded to anyone else (see BOP).

Spammer: Someone who sends repeated text messages to others in an annoying manner.

Spawn: See Pop.

Spec: See Build.

Sploit: Exploit. See Dupe for an example.

Squishy: A character who cannot take significant damage (relative to others) and survive; often the casting classes who wear cloth armor.

ST: Secondary Tank. See OT.

STFU: Shut The F*** Up.

STR: Strength.

Stun: A type of CC.

SWG: Star Wars Galaxies, a Sci-Fi MMORPG.

Tank: See Meat Shield.

Taunt: An ability (often used by Tanks) to draw a monster's aggro.

Tell: A private message to another person in the game.

Tick (Tic/Tik): A small period of time in the game (it could be one second).

Toon: Cartoon. Another word for a player's character or avatar.

Train: When a group of monsters is chasing a player.

Trash: Monsters that are very easy to kill and often don't yield anything of use.

Trolling: Purposefully writing irritating posts in hopes of starting a flame war.

Twink: A low level character with powerful gear handed to him by a higher level character. Also can be synonymous with power-leveling.

TY: Thank you.

Uber: Super or very powerful.

UO: Ultima Online, an MMORPG.

Vendor: An NPC merchant that buys and sells items to players.

Vendor Trash: An item that a player doesn't want (and should probably sell to a vendor for money).

Vent: Ventrilo. A popular software program that allows players to talk to each other over the internet (rather than type).

Vuln: Vulnerable.

WB: Welcome Back.

Whisper: See Tell.

Wiped: When everyone in the party is killed.

WOOT: Horray!

WOW: World Of Warcraft, an MMORPG.

WTB: Want To Buy.

WTC: Want To Craft.

WTF: What The F***?

WTS: Want To Sell.

WTT: Want To Trade.

XP: See Experience.

Yellow: See Con.

Zerg/Zerging: To attack something with a lot of force, often with little strategy.

Zone: A distinct area in the game. Also can be used as "Zone!," which means "leave the area immediately."

Index